Developing **literacy** Skills

Through History

KEY STAGE 2: Y5–6

Christine Moorcroft

HOPSCOTCH
EDUCATIONAL PUBLISHING

✦ Contents ✦

Published by Hopscotch Publishing Ltd,
29 Waterloo Place, Leamington Spa CV32 5LA.
(Tel: 01926 744227)

© 2001 Hopscotch Educational Publishing

Written by Christine Moorcroft
Series design by Blade Communications
Illustrated by Dave Burroughs
Cover illustrated by Susan Hutchinson
Printed by Clintplan, Southam

Christine Moorcroft hereby asserts her moral right to be
identified as the author of this work in accordance with
the Copyright, Designs and Patents Act, 1988.

ISBN 1-902239-77-6

Introduction

 ## ABOUT THE SERIES

Developing Literacy Skills Through History is a series of books aimed at developing key literacy skills using a range of written genres based on a history theme, from Key Stage 1 (P1–3) through to Key Stage 2 (P4–7).

The series offers a structured approach which provides detailed lesson plans to teach specific literacy and history skills. A unique feature of the series is the provision of differentiated photocopiable activities aimed at considerably reducing teacher preparation time. Suggestions for follow-up activities for both literacy and history ensure maximum use of this resource.

ABOUT THIS BOOK

This book is for teachers of children at Key Stage 2, Years 5–6 and Scottish levels P6–7. It aims to:

+ develop children's literacy and history skills through exposure to and experience of a wide range of stimulating texts with supporting differentiated activities which are both diversified and challenging
+ support teachers by providing practical teaching methods based on whole-class, group, paired and individual teaching
+ encourage enjoyment and curiosity as well as develop skills of interpretation and response.

 ## CHAPTER CONTENT

 ### Literacy objectives

This outlines the aims for the literacy activities suggested in the lesson plan.

History objectives

This outlines the history learning objectives that relate to the lesson plan.

 ### Resources

This lists the different resources that the teacher needs to teach the lesson.

 ### Starting point: Whole class

This provides ideas for introducing the activity and may include key questions to ask the children.

 ### Using the photocopiable text

This explains how to use the provided text extract with the children as a shared reading activity and introduction to the group work. It may also be used by groups during the group work.

 ### Group activities

This explains how to use each sheet as well as providing guidance on the type of child who will benefit most from each sheet.

 ### Plenary session

This suggests ideas for whole-class sessions to discuss the learning outcomes and follow-up work.

 ### Follow-up ideas for literacy

This contains suggestions for further literacy activities related to the lesson plan, which can be carried out at another time.

 ### Follow-up ideas for history

This contains suggestions for further history activities which might be carried out at another time or during a designated history lesson.

Victorian children at work

Literacy objectives

- ✦ To understand the basic conventions of standard English. (Y5, T1: S2)
- ✦ To revise the function of pronouns and agreement between nouns, pronouns and verbs. (Y5, T2: S4)
- ✦ To understand how words vary across dialects. (Y5, T3: W9)

History objectives

(Unit 11)
- ✦ To find out about the everyday lives of Victorian children.
- ✦ To understand the attitudes of people of the time towards children.
- ✦ To use different sources to find information about a period in history.

Resources

- ✦ Information books about Victorian children at work.
- ✦ Engravings and paintings of Victorian children at work.
- ✦ Leaflets about present-day legislation on children at work.

Starting point: Whole class

- ✦ Ask the children what they know about the ages at which children are expected to start school and at what ages they can go to work. What kinds of jobs do school children do in their spare time? Discuss jobs in which children have an employer (for example, newspaper rounds and milk deliveries) and work which they find for themselves (for example, washing cars, helping members of their families with work in the home and odd jobs for friends and neighbours).
- ✦ Explain the legal aspects of employing children, such as maximum hours and the types of work which are allowed or prohibited. Say that there are laws which limit the hours and types of work that children of different ages can do. Show them leaflets about children at work.
- ✦ Explain that in the early eighteenth century children from poor families worked from the age of five (sometimes even three) in places such as iron-mines and coalmines, cotton- and woollen mills, nail and match factories, gas-works and farms; others worked at home

or on the streets, doing work such as weaving, making nails, carrying bags, sweeping the streets and selling things. Boys were employed as chimney-sweeps.
- ✦ Show the children etchings and paintings of Victorian children at work and books containing information about the employment laws, such as those passed in 1802 and 1819 (limiting children's work in cotton-mills, but not in other places, to 12 hours per day), the 'Ten-Hour Act' of 1847 (which limited the work of women and children to 10 hours per day) and the Factory Act of 1874 (which banned anyone under the age of 14 from full-time work). Compare this with present-day regulations. The children should realise that the working day of most adults nowadays is only about eight hours.

Using the photocopiable text

- ✦ Enlarge the class text or make a copy for each child.
- ✦ Explain that the text was written by a Victorian journalist who interviewed children who worked in the streets, markets and other places in London. The boy in the text lived wherever he could find shelter; his parents had died.
- ✦ Share the text and ask them to notice how any unusual spellings help them to pronounce the words in the way the boy spoke. How can they tell which words are spoken by the children and which by the journalist?
- ✦ Discuss any dialects with which the children are familiar, the different pronunciation for certain words and the slang terms used. Point out that in everyday conversation (and in plays, novels and poems) dialect and slang words are acceptable but that for more formal writing, standard English should be used so that everyone is clear as to what it means. To demonstrate this, give them examples from a dialect and ask them if they can understand it. For example, 'Gizzago' – 'May I have a turn?' (Liverpool)
- ✦ What examples of non-standard English can they find in the shared text, including dialect words? Highlight them. Point out the occasional addition of the letter 'h' at the beginning of a word ('hinterested' and 'heels') as well as the lack of it at the beginning of words where it should be. Find examples of inconsistency between verbs and pronouns ('I gets', 'I has'). Model how this would be written in standard English. Look at dialect and slang words such as 'yarned' for 'earned' and 'stunnin', for 'lovely' or 'splendid'.

Note: There should be no suggestion that non-standard English is inferior to standard English. Each has its place.

Victorian children at work

 ## Group activities

Activity sheet 1: This is for children who are beginning to recognise non-standard English, including agreement between nouns or pronouns and verbs, and the ways in which the past tenses of verbs are formed.

Activity sheet 2: This is for children who recognise the differences between standard and non-standard English, including agreement between nouns or pronouns and verbs, and the ways in which the past tenses of verbs are formed. They also understand that dialects use words that are not standard English and are used in written English only when they represent the way someone speaks.

Activity sheet 3: This is for children who can recognise different aspects of non-standard English, including dialect words, phrases and non-standard grammar. They understand the use of non-standard spelling to indicate pronunciation.

 ## Plenary session

✦ Display an enlarged copy of the class text or ask the children to look at their own copies of it. Begin with the children who completed Activity sheet 1 and invite them to share their responses. Move on to Activity sheet 2 and encourage the children to look in the class text for similar expressions to those on their sheet. For example, what word does the boy use for 'man'? What does he say instead of 'an old woman'? What expression does he use for 'eating'?

✦ Reread the text with the children, underlining or highlighting each example of non-standard English. Ask some of the children who completed Activity sheet 3 to read their rewritten version of the text on the sheet.

 ## Follow-up ideas for literacy

✦ The children could 'translate' the whole passage into standard English and read it aloud. Compare the new version with the original – which is better for its purpose, and why?

✦ The children could make dictionaries of dialect words for a dialect they know well (either a local dialect or one they hear frequently on television). They could include other frequently-heard examples of non-standard English, such as lack of agreement between nouns or pronouns and verbs, inconsistency of tense and subject, unconventional formation of tenses (for example, 'I give' for 'I gave') and double negatives.

✦ During their work in history (see below) the children should make a note of any new or technical words they come across, find their meanings and collect them to make a glossary. Useful reference books include *The Shorter Oxford Dictionary*, dictionaries of slang words and etymological dictionaries.

 ## Follow-up ideas for history

✦ What does the text tell the children about life in Victorian London and about the care of children? They could organise their responses under headings such as 'the streets', 'work' and 'money'. What does it tell them about the attitudes of people at the time towards children? Draw out the idea of the need for children from poor families to earn money, and ask what differences there are nowadays.

✦ Discuss the types of information they can gather from different sources: journalistic (such as *London Labour and the London Poor* by Henry Mayhew), official reports (such as parliamentary reports) and the extract, plus fiction such as *Her Benny* by Silas Hocking and *The Water Babies* by Charles Kingsley.

✦ Using material from local art galleries, museums, libraries, CD-Roms and the Internet, the children could research the work of Victorian children. Each group could research a different type of work – on farms, in factories, in coalmines, tin or lead mines, in woollen and cotton mills, at home (for example, weaving or making nails), as servants or on the streets. They could write a non-chronological report by an 'inspector' saying what they have discovered about the work of children at the time.

Another boy … gave me the following account:

"The fust browns as I ivver yarned," he said, "was from a drover going into the country … and had to carry some passels for somebody down there. They wasn't 'evvy, but they was orkerd to grip. His old 'oman luk out for a young cove to 'elp her old man, and saw me fust, so she calls me and I gets the job. I gived the greatest of satisfaction, and had sixpence giv me, for Jim [the drover] was well paid, as they was vallyble passels …

"I used to carry his tea from his old 'oman," he went on, "to a old cove as had a stunnin' pitch of fruit in the City-road. But my best friend was Stumpy; he had a beautiful crossin' [as a sweeper] then, but he's dead now and berried as well. I used to talk to him and whistle – I can just whistle" [here he whistled loud and shrill, to convince me of his perfection in the street accomplishment] " – and to dance him the double-shuffle" [he favoured me with a specimen of that dance], "and he said I hinterested him. Well, he meant he liked it, I s'pose. When he went to rest I had his crossin' and his broom for nuffin'. One boy used to say to Stumpy, 'I'll give you 1d for your crossin' while you's grubbin'.' But I had it for nuffin', and had all I yarned; sometimes 1d, sometimes 2d, but only once 3½d. I've been 'elping Old Bill with his summer cabbages and flowers [cauliflowers] and now he's on live heels. I can sing 'em out prime, but you 'eared me. I has my bit o' grub with him, and a few browns … I've cried for an' 'elped other costers. Stumpy sent me to 'em … I'll go for some bunse soon. I don't know what I shall do time to come, I nivver thinks on it. I could read middlin', and can a little now, but I'm out of practice."

	Glossary
browns	copper coins, usually halfpennies
bunse	poor quality apples sold off cheaply, or even given, to market-boys, who could sell them for a small profit
cove	man
crossin'	part of a street which was kept clean by a crossing-sweeper so that people could cross without dirtying their shoes in mud, horse droppings or rubbish. People gave the crossing-sweepers a penny or two in return.
1d	one (old) penny (240 old pence = £1)
yarned	earned

◆ Non-standard English ◆

✦ Write the correct forms of the verbs.

The parcels _____ heavy.

| wasn't/ weren't |

We _____ sweeping the street.

| was/were |

I never _____ about this.

| think/thinks |

I _____ plenty of work here.

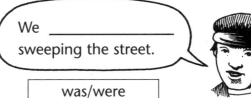

| have/has |

✦ Now write the past tense correctly.

She _____ out for a young man to help.

| look/looked/luk |

I _____ the job.

| gets/got/gotten |

She saw me and _____ me.

| call/calls/called |

You _____ me.

| heard/hearded |

✦ Write this sentence correctly.

I gived the greatest of satisfaction, and had sixpence giv me.

_____

◆ Non-standard English ◆

✦ Write the correct forms of the verbs in this passage.

All my sisters has/have _____ been hurriers, but three work/worked _____ in the mill. Alice went/goed _____ to the mill because her legs swelled/swollen/swoll _____ from hurrying in cold water when she were/was/are _____ hot.

I never went to day school. I go/goes _____ to Sunday school but I canna/can't _____ read or write.

I go to the pit at five o'clock in the morning. I get/gets/getting _____ my breakfast [porridge and milk] first: I takes/take/taken _____ my dinner with me, a cake, and eaten/eats/eat _____ it as I work; I don't/doesn't/dinna _____ stop for a rest or anything else. The next meal is/are/am _____ when I get home at five in the evening, potatoes and sometimes meat.

I work/works _____ in the clothes I've got on, trousers and a jacket. The bald place on my head is/are _____ from hurrying the corves [baskets]. I hurry/hurries _____ eleven a day a mile or more underground, and back. They weighs/weigh/weight _____ three hundredweights. I wear/wears/wearing _____ a chain and belt at the workings to get the corves out.

The men are naked except for their caps. If I am/is/are _____ not quick enough they beat/beats _____ me; they strike/strikes _____ me on the back with their hands.

✦ On the back of this sheet write these sentences in standard English.

I canna say how many children work here. The lasses dinna like it.
They get beat if they's no quick enough.

◆ Non-standard English ◆

◆ Read the text below. Underline the different
kinds of non-standard English:
    verbs not matching pronouns (red)
    dialect words (blue)
    unusual spellings (green)

"Oh, Nell!" Benny burst out, "I's just soft, I is. I's missed a hour in the time. I never did think I was such a fool. But it can't be helped now, nohow."

"I was afraid you'd got hurt, Benny," said Nelly.

"Me hurt? Never fear! I knows how to take care of myself. But what luck, Nell?"

"Bad, Benny, very bad. Nobody wanted matches today."

"By golly, Nell! What's us to do? You heard the guv'nor this morning?"

"Ay," said Nelly. "But 'ave you 'ad bad luck too?"

"Horful, Nell – simply horful!"

Just then a gentleman was seen crossing the street with a portmanteau.

"Here's a gent with a portmantle," whispered Benny to his sister. "I'll try my luck! Foller me, Nell, as quick as you can." And off he darted.

"Carry yer bag, sir?" he said, stepping in front of the gentleman. The gentleman looked kindly down into the two honest-looking eyes that flashed in the gaslight.

"What will you take the bag to the ferry for?" he inquired.

"For what you please to give," said Benny sturdily. "Times is bad at present, and little chaps like us is glad to 'ave what we catches."

"Oh, that's it, is it? But I'm afraid this bag is too heavy for you."

"Oh, never fear," said Benny, as he got hold of the portmanteau. "I's 'mazing strong, and ken carry this like winkin'."

From *Her Benny*, by Silas Hocking, 1880, based on real children in Liverpool.

◆ Now, on another sheet of paper, rewrite the text using standard English.

Chapter 2

Victorian children at play

 Literacy objectives

+ To identify the imperative form in instructional writing and to use this awareness in own writing. (Y5, T1: S9)
+ To write instructional texts. (Y5, T1: T25)
+ To prepare for reading by identifying what they already know and what they need to find out. (Y5, T2: T16)
+ To revise the language conventions and grammatical features of instructional texts. (Y6, T3: S1)

 History objectives

(Unit 11)
+ To consider what life was like for Victorian children.

 Resources

+ Information books (with pictures) about children's games in Victorian times.
+ Paintings of Victorian children at play.
+ Copies of instructions for games.

 Starting point: Whole class

+ Show the children the copies of paintings of poor, middle-class and rich Victorian children at play (indoors and outdoors). For example, 'Children at Play' (John Dawson Watson), 'Bubbles' (Sir John Everett Millais), 'Her Idol' (W Q Orchardson), 'The Lowther Arcade' (H C Bryant) and 'The Garden Seat' (Kate Greenaway). Ask them to describe what the children are doing and any toys or other equipment they are using in their games (for example, hoops, balls, bats, tops and whips). Are the games being played by the children in the pictures similar to any games played today?
+ The children could explain why certain games could not have been played in Victorian times and comment on the toys that were not available then (for example, computer games and other electronic games). They could also discuss what made the playing of certain games easier then than it is now. For example, children in towns could play in the streets because there was less traffic and it moved much more slowly than it does today.
+ Discuss the differences between the games played by poor, middle-class and rich children. Rich children had far more toys of different kinds but they would not have been allowed to play in the streets or fields and so their

games were solitary or shared with brothers and sisters. Poor children's families could not afford to buy toys for them; they had home-made toys such as rag-dolls, metal hoops, tops and whips (these were sometimes made from bobbins from the cotton- and woollen mills), and they usually played in the streets and fields rather than inside their homes. Middle-class children had fewer toys than the rich and were unlikely to be allowed to play in the streets or fields.

Using the photocopiable text

+ Enlarge the class text or make a copy for each child.
+ Tell the children they are going to share a text about a game called 'hopscotch'. Have they ever played this game? What would they like to find out about the game? List their questions on the board.
+ Tell the children the derivation of the word 'hopscotch'. 'Scotch' was a late Middle English word for 'scratch' or 'score' and came to be used specifically for the 'scratched' lines of a hopscotch grid.
+ Now share the text with the children. Ask them in what kind of book they think they might find text of this type (an information book about history or games).
+ Which of the children's questions did the text answer? What were the answers? Write them in note form on the board under the questions.
+ Ask the children what the readers need to know before they begin playing (the equipment they need and how to mark out the playing area). Point out that the readers need to be told the object of the game – how to win.
+ Explain that they are going to write some instructions for the game. How are game instructions usually set out? Look at some examples and compare the layouts, for example whether numbering or bullet points are used. Point out the use of the imperative form of the verbs at the beginning of sentences, such as 'Shuffle the cards' or 'Shake the dice'.
+ Ask the children to tell you how they think they could convert the class text into instructions. Discuss the sentences and the form of the verbs. They are statements of what was (or is) done and the verbs are in the indicative mood (for example, 'The player throws a pebble'). How should the verbs be changed so that the sentences sound like instructions (imperatives)? (The verbs should be changed to the imperative mood, for example 'Throw a pebble …', 'Hop to the area …')

Victorian children at play

 ## Group activities

Activity sheet 1: This is for children who are beginning to understand the features of an instructional text. They know that instructions often begin with a list of equipment and that they should be written in the correct order. They are beginning to recognise the imperative form of verbs.

Activity sheet 2: This is for children who recognise the distinctive features of instructions. With support, they can identify the relevant information from another source and present it in the form of instructions.

Activity sheet 3: This is for children who understand the conventions of layout, order and language of instructions and can convert a descriptive passage into a set of instructions.

 ## Plenary session

✦ Display an enlarged copy of the text (on page 12) or ask the children to look at their own copies of it. Begin with the children who completed Activity sheet 1 and ask them to read the instructions in the correct order. The others should listen and comment on any points which they think are out of sequence. Move on to Activity sheets 2 and 3 and invite some of the children who completed them to read out their instructions while the others try to follow them. During a subsequent lesson the children could edit and improve their instructions.

 ## Follow-up ideas for literacy

✦ Display pictures of Victorian children at play, and information books about their games and toys. Encourage the class to make notes about their observations of these games and toys. They could think of questions regarding the games and toys and research the answers. They could write headings under which to organise their notes, for example 'Outdoor games', 'Indoor games', 'Poor children at play', 'Rich children at play'.

✦ The children could find out about specific toys that interest them (for example, mechanical toys, hobby-horses or dolls) and do some research on them using more specialised books or the websites of museums (see page 64). Ask them to draw the toy and make notes about how it was used and which children would have played with it (rich, poor or middle-class). They could use their notes and drawings to prepare cues for a talk to the rest of the class about their chosen game or toy.

✦ The children could write instructions for using one of their own toys and then alter the instructions so that a Victorian child would understand them. Ask them to identify things that Victorian children would not know about and then suggest ways in which they could be helped to understand them.

✦ The children's instructions for the game of hopscotch could be displayed on a 'How to play' board, to which they could add instructions for playing other games.

 ## Follow-up ideas for history

✦ The children could discuss the ways in which they spend their spare time, and list the hobbies and interests of their group. Ask them to organise their hobbies and interests on a chart, indicating whether or not these would have been possible in Victorian times (and the reasons why).

✦ Tell the children about some of the Victorian attitudes to children. For example, that they should learn moral principles. They could find out more about this from popular Victorian nursery rhymes and from websites and textbooks about education in Victorian times.

How we spend our spare time			
Possible in Victorian times	Why	Not possible in Victorian times	Why

Hopscotch

The game of hopscotch (which is still played) was very popular in Victorian times. It was played in the street and school playgrounds. It was for any number of players from one to about six.

In Victorian times children used to scratch the numbers for a hopscotch grid on to paving stones, or they would use a stick to draw the grid and numbers on a flat piece of ground.

The first player stands behind the starting line and throws a stone into the area marked '1'. If the stone lands in area 1, the player hops to it, lands on one foot, picks it up and returns, hopping, to the starting point.

After that the player throws the stone into area 2, hops to it, picks it up and hops back to the starting point. He or she can hop into area 1, using it as a 'stepping-stone'.

Next, the player throws the stone into area 3, hops to it, picks it up and hops back to the starting point (using areas 1 and 2 as stepping-stones, if necessary), and so on.

The player continues until he or she reaches 'out' or commits a 'foul'. The following are fouls:

● throwing the stone into the wrong area, or off the grid
● hopping on to a line
● having both feet on the ground at once.

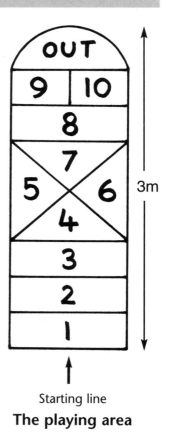

3m

Starting line
The playing area

On their second, third and fourth turns, and so on, the players try to throw the stone into whichever area they were trying for when their last turn ended.

The winner is the first to throw a stone into 'out', hop to it, pick it up and hop back to the starting point (using the other areas as stepping-stones, but without committing any fouls).

◆ Writing instructions ◆

✦ Cut out the instructions for playing hopscotch and arrange them in the correct order. Number the instructions.

Hop back to the starting point. You can use area 1 as a 'stepping-stone'.

Pick up the stone and hop back to the starting point.

Throw the stone into area 2.

Continue until you reach 'out' or commit a 'foul'.

On your second, third and fourth turn and so on, throw the stone into whichever area you were trying for when your last turn ended.

On your first turn, stand behind the starting line and throw a stone into area 1.

Do not:
• throw the stone into the wrong area or off the grid
• hop on to a line
• put both feet on the ground.

These are 'fouls'.

Hop to area 2 and pick up the stone. You can use area 1 as a 'stepping-stone'.

Hop back to the starting point. You can use areas 1 and 2 as 'stepping-stones'.

Next throw the stone into area 3.

Hop to area 1, landing on one foot.

To win, be the first to throw a stone into 'out', hop to it, pick up the stone and hop back over the starting line. Use other areas as 'stepping-stones' but do not commit any 'fouls'.

If the stone lands in area 3, hop to it and pick it up. You can use areas 1 and 2 as 'stepping-stones'.

You need:
  a stone
  a playing area marked
    like this:

✦ Writing instructions ✦

✦ Write instructions for playing hopscotch.

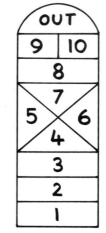

The playing area

Equipment
_____
_____

Number of players _____

How to play

1. Stand behind the starting line and throw the stone
_____

2. Hop to _____ and _____

3. Hop back_____

4. Throw _____

5. Hop _____

6. You can _____

7. Throw _____

8. Hop _____

9. Hop _____

10. Continue until you _____ or _____

11. Stop, and let the other players _____

12. On your next turn _____

13. To win you must _____

Fouls

• _____

_____

_____

• _____

_____

• _____

_____

◆ Writing instructions ◆

◆ Write instructions for playing hopscotch.

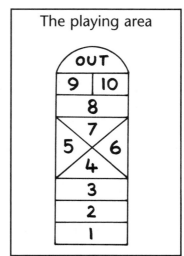

The playing area

Equipment

_____

_____

Number of players _____

How to play

_____

_____

_____

Tell the players what to do on each turn. Number the instructions.

_____

_____

Explain what a foul is.

_____

_____

_____

_____

Explain how they know when their turn ends.

_____

_____

Explain how to win.

_____

Continue on the back of the sheet if you need to.

Chapter 3

The effects of the railways

 Literacy objectives

- To construct an argument in note form or full text to persuade others of a point of view. (Y5, T3: T19)
- To investigate connecting words and phrases. (Y6, T1: S4)
- To recognise how arguments are constructed to be effective. (Y6, T2: T15)
- To identify the features of balanced arguments. (Y6, T2: T16)
- To construct effective arguments. (Y6, T2: T18)

 History objectives

(Unit 12)
- To describe the attitudes of different people to the building of a railway.
- To communicate their understanding of the advantages and disadvantages of railways.

 Resources

- Engravings and paintings of goods, livestock and passenger transport in early Victorian times (particularly in the local area) including stagecoaches, horses and carts, people on horseback, people on foot on country roads, cattle drovers and canals.

 Starting point: Whole class

- Show the children the pictures of the transport of goods, livestock and people before the advent of railways. Discuss the different opportunities enjoyed by people from different walks of life, and the limitations for people who did not own a carriage or horse and could not afford stagecoach fares.
- Tell the children about the increase in industry in Britain during the Industrial Revolution. For example, the rise in the production of textiles, such as wool, cotton and silk, and the growth of manufacturing based on iron and steel. Explain the role played by steam in industry and the need for coal to power steam engines. Tell them that roads at the time were little more than dirt tracks; they were dusty in the summer and muddy in the winter, criss-crossed with ruts from cartwheels and pitted by horses' hooves. Also explain to them that the building of canals had made a big difference to the transport of heavy goods, such as coal, but that canal transport was very slow and there were tolls to be paid as well as the carrier's charges.

- Ask the children how the increase in industry affected the area in which they live. For example, is there evidence of Victorian factories or mills in the area?

 Using the photocopiable text

- Enlarge the class text on page 18 or make a copy for each child.
- After reading the passage with the children, tell them that they are going to collect information to help them write an argument showing the views of different people on the building of railways. Model how to identify and mark the parts of the text that provide the kind of information they need (which groups of people are mentioned, whether they would welcome the railway and why or why not). Show the children how to record their notes under the headings 'for' and 'against'. You could extend this by asking them what other kinds of information would help them to plan their argument (for example, about other people the railway affected) and where they could find it.
- Discuss the characteristics of an argument. It argues for or against something, supporting opinions with evidence. It acknowledges other points of view and answers them. Read an argument to the children, perhaps from a newspaper, and ask them to point out the tense and person it is written in and to identify the evidence used to support the opinions expressed.
- Ask the children to identify the points made for and against a proposal or issue and to say which view the argument favours. Point out the summary and conclusion.
- Draw attention to the logical connectives used to link the points made. For example, 'although', 'but', 'by the same token', 'despite that', 'however', 'moreover', 'on the other hand', 'surely' and 'to conclude'. The children could compare these with the connectives used to indicate the passage of time in chronological reports ('next', 'then', 'afterwards' and 'after that').

 Group activities

Activity sheet 1: This is for children who are beginning to recognise the differences between an argument and other texts. They know that an argument presents different points of view and can recognise which of these support or oppose the proposal.

Activity sheet 2: This is for children who can extract from a passage the points of view of different people and identify the arguments against a proposal and those that can be

Literacy through history

KS2: Y5–6

The effects of the railways

used to counter them. They could continue the activity on the back of the sheet or on another piece of paper.

Activity sheet 3: This is for children who understand the structure of an argument. They can select evidence from a passage to support or oppose the issue being argued and are learning to use connectives to structure their argument.

 Plenary session

✦ Display an enlarged copy of the text on page 18 or ask the children to look at their own copies. Begin with those who completed Activity sheet 1 and invite them to share their responses. Ask who supported/opposed the introduction of railways and the reasons why. Can they think of any other people who might have supported or opposed the building of railways? Ask them to express some of the arguments that these people might use.

✦ Ask the children who completed Activity sheet 2 to read out their arguments for and against the building of railways. Help them to write a conclusion and to use appropriate connectives to lead on to the conclusion. For example, 'to sum up', 'in conclusion', 'overall' and 'it is clear that'.

✦ Invite some of the children who completed Activity sheet 3 to read out their argument, while the others listen for the use of logical connectives. List these and discuss how they were useful in the argument.

 Follow-up ideas for literacy

✦ The children could read other arguments and make a note of the logical connectives they come across. They could compile a class word bank of logical connectives, using a word-processed table to order it alphabetically.

✦ Introduce an issue which is relevant to the children (perhaps one that has been in the news). Ask them for their views on it and list these in note form on an overhead transparency. Make a photocopy of it for each group and ask the groups to cut out and organise the opinions under the headings 'For' and 'Against'. They should then fill out the notes into connected prose. Help them to structure the class's views as an argument, encouraging them to collect evidence from printed and electronic sources.

✦ Investigate the use of conditionals in arguments, such as 'if …then', 'might', 'could' or 'would', and the way in which they can be used to introduce speculation. The children could identify any conditionals which they used in their arguments about the railways and edit their writing if they find any incorrect verbs forms.

 Follow-up ideas for history

✦ Investigate the direct and indirect effects of the development of railways on the local area. The following points should be considered: railway lines and stations (used and disused), the development of industries, the decline of any local employment or business, the existence of any drovers' roads and what happened to them after railways came into use, the development (or change of location) of livestock markets and the decline or development of inns and guest-houses.

✦ The children could use local libraries, museums and the Internet to research the growth or decline of a specific business in the locality in Victorian times. For example, a local farm, shop, manufacturer or service, such as an inn or transport business. Each group could research one business and write a report that describes and explains its development or decline during Victorian times.

A mine-owner in 1825 argues for a railway

We need a railway to link Shildon and other collieries in West Durham with the port of Stockton-on-Tees. We cannot easily transport our coal from our inland collieries to the coast and, from there, to the rest of the country by sea.

Our problem is that the only forms of transport we have for goods are pack-horses and horse-drawn carts. They cannot carry very large or heavy loads.

A map of Britain showing the location of Shildon

It is 25 miles from Witton Park to Stockton, and a pack-horse cannot carry a heavy load of coal over that distance without many stops for resting. In addition to that, the load carried would be too small to be worth selling. We need quick transport for very large, heavy loads. Moreover, a cart is of little use, even though it allows a horse to carry a greater load, because the roads are so bad. A cart can barely travel a mile without breaking a wheel in a rut in the road.

Although a canal has been suggested, it would not be a good idea to build it because of the huge cost. A railway, however, would be much cheaper. Another advantage is that a railway would be quicker to build.

More importantly, faster transport for heavier loads would enable us to sell much more coal than we do now. The advantage of this would be to bring down the price of coal, not only for businesses but also for the public. Local people here in Shildon could find the cost of running their households much reduced.

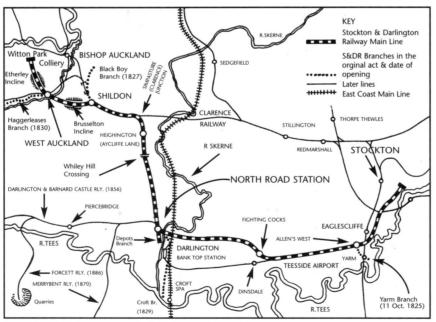

A map showing the railways built around Stockton and Darlington in the 1820s

It would not just be the collieries which would benefit; think of all the other businesses along the route. They, too, would have access to quick, cheap transport. They would prosper and their success would provide work for more people in the district.

To conclude, the building of a railway from Shildon to Stockton would have huge benefits for the collieries, local businesses and the general public of West Durham.

◆ For or against the railway ◆

◆ Read what these Victorian people had to say about the building of a new railway.
Write 'For' or 'Against' next to each one. Then complete the chart.

The railway will carry goods cheaply and quickly to the port.

A factory owner

I don't want my land damaged by a noisy railway.

A landowner

The railway will provide a much quicker and cheaper way of getting my cattle to the market than having a drover walk them there.

A farmer

I, and others like me, will be out of work before long.

A cattle drover

Our village is going to be spoiled by all these day-trippers and weekend visitors.

A resident of Blackpool

Our business will do well.

Innkeeper at Whitby

We shall lose customers. We might have to close down.

The keeper of a coaching inn

Our iron and steel are going to be needed.

Steelworks owner

It will put us out of business.

Canal-boat owner

Arguing for the railway	Arguing against the railway

Continue on the other side of the sheet if necessary.

For or against the railway

✦ Read the passage below. It tells us how the coming of the railways affected different people.

- Railways can carry coal from the coalfields to the ports.

- The trade of ship-owners is growing, but the canals will be used less and less for the transport of coal.

- Railways bring raw materials from the ports to the factories and carry manufactured goods to the ports cheaply and quickly. The factories are prospering and providing employment for people in towns.

- The railways also create employment for engine-drivers, guards, porters, track-layers, labourers and so on.

- Passengers are using stagecoaches less and less and the coaching inns are losing trade.

- Inns and guest-houses are springing up in seaside villages now that many more people can afford to go for day trips and weekend outings.

- Farmers are able to transport their livestock by rail, instead of paying a drover to walk them for miles to the markets.

✦ Imagine you are a railway builder. How would you answer the arguments against railways? Write both sides of the argument in the speech bubbles.

Arguments against railways   The railway builder's answers

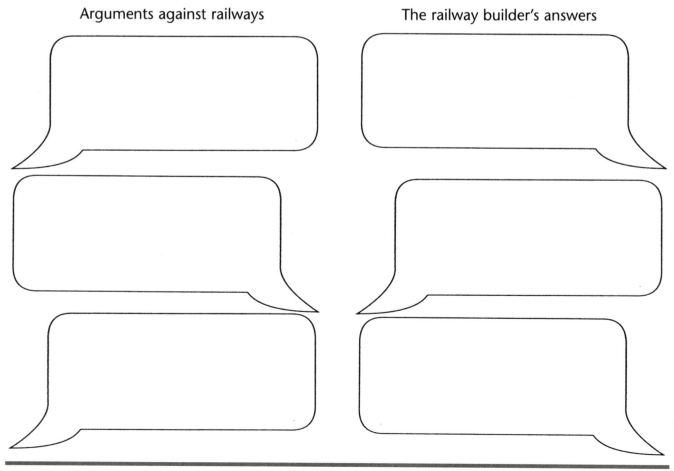

For or against the railway

✦ Read the text below about how the coming of the railways affected different people.

> Railways can carry coal from the coalfields to the ports. The trade of ship-owners is growing, but the canals will be used less and less for the transport of coal. Railways bring raw materials from the ports to the factories and carry manufactured goods to the ports cheaply and quickly. The factories are prospering and providing employment for people in towns. The railways also create employment for engine-drivers, guards, porters, track-layers, labourers and so on. Passengers are using stagecoaches less and less and the coaching inns are losing trade. Inns and guest-houses are springing up in seaside villages now that many more people can afford to go for day trips and weekend outings. Farmers are able to transport their livestock by rail, instead of paying a drover to walk them for miles to the markets.

✦ Imagine you are a railway builder. How would you answer the arguments against railways? Plan an argument to support the building of a railway.

The building of this railway will enable coal to be transported _____

_____

In addition, raw materials _____

_____

Another benefit _____

_____

Although drovers _____

_____

Moreover, farmers _____

Also _____

Despite the complaints of _____

_____

In conclusion, _____

_____

Continue on the other side of the sheet if necessary.

Chapter 4

1950s' home entertainment

 ## Literacy objectives

+ To understand how words and expressions have changed over time. (Y6, T1: W7)
+ To make notes. (Y5, T1: T26)
+ To prepare for reading by identifying what they already know and what they need to find out. (Y5, T2: T16)

 ## History objectives

(Unit 13)
+ To learn about the changes that have occurred to the way of life of people in Britain since 1948.
+ To identify a range of appropriate sources of information.

 ## Resources

+ Information books about the 1950s.
+ A 1950s' radio and television set (or replicas or pictures of them).
+ Pictures of 1950s' families watching television and listening to the radio.
+ Music records from the 1950s and, if possible, a radiogram.

 ## Starting point: Whole class

+ Show the children radio and television sets and a radiogram from the 1950s and discuss the similarities and differences with their modern counterparts. Point out the controls, the flex and the plug (probably a small, round-pin plug and a double, twisted flex covered with rubber and a brown cotton outer coating). Discuss the materials from which the equipment is made and its design.
+ Look at pictures of families watching television and listening to the radio. How is this different from today? Discuss the ways in which modern children watch

television. Do they have more than one television at home? In which rooms? How many radios do they have? Where do they and their families listen to them (in the bathroom, in the garden, outdoors and so on)?
+ Ask the children how they decide which programmes to watch on television and what they do if everyone wants to watch different programmes. What happens when there are two or three programmes that they want to watch which are all on at the same time?
+ Look at the music records from the 1950s (78s) and compare them with the compact discs of today. The children might also mention cassette tapes. Tell them that these were not available in the 1950s, although some people had reel-to-reel tape recorders. (The children could find out about these.) If possible, play some 1950s' records and compare them with popular music of today.

Using the photocopiable text

+ Enlarge the class text on page 24 or make a copy for each child.
+ Share the text with the children and ask them to underline and identify any unfamiliar words. List these words. Which of them are explained in the text? Examples include 'wireless', 'radiogram' and '78 record'. Discuss the words that are not explained. What can the children deduce about them from their context? Discuss how some of these words have changed over time. Why did the word 'wireless' stop being used? What other words do they know of that have become unfashionable? Model the use of different types of dictionary to find the meanings of the unfamiliar words, for example *The New Shorter Oxford Dictionary*, *Brewer's Dictionary of Phrase and Fable* and scientific and technological dictionaries.
+ Discuss what the children now know about home entertainment in the 1950s. Write their responses on a flow chart, such as the one below.

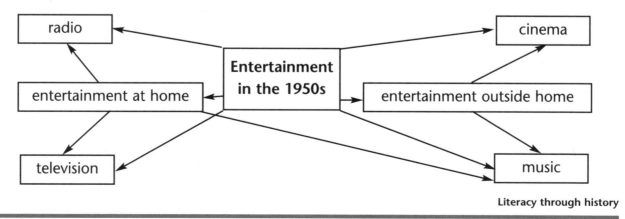

Literacy through history

KS2: Y5–6

1950s' home entertainment

✦ To prepare the children for the activity sheets, you may need to revise note-taking: omitting unnecessary words and using abbreviations.

 ## Group activities

Activity sheet 1: This is for children who need guidance in identifying what they already know about a topic. In this case the topic is 'radio'. It provides prompts as to what they should write about 1950s' radio by asking them to compare it with present-day radio. They also begin to recognise what they do not know.

Activity sheet 2: This is for children who, with the help of a structured table, can identify what they know about a topic. They can recognise what they need to find out and can suggest sources to use.

Activity sheet 3: This is for children who can select a sub-topic from a broader topic and then identify what they know about it. They can decide what else they need to find out, list each aspect of this in an organised way and suggest the most appropriate sources.

 ## Plenary session

Photocopy each activity sheet on to an OHT or make enlarged copies. Invite the children to read from Activity sheet 1. Fill in their responses and ask the others to add suggestions as to what could be found out about each topic. Repeat this process for Activity sheets 2 and 3. Discuss the ways in which the notes were made on Activity sheet 3. Can the children suggest ways in which to improve this? Examples include finding ways in which to speed up and organise note-taking by the use of abbreviations, arrows and boxes, and the omission of unnecessary words.

 ## Follow-up ideas for literacy

✦ The children could prepare a five-minute talk on what they have found out during their work on 1950s' home entertainment. Encourage them to think of an interesting opening to engage the interest of their audience. They could practise reading their prepared talk to a partner, who could time it. Suggest ways in which they could edit and refine their talk and ask them to think of a summary or final comment that will leave their audience with a question or something to think about.

✦ Discuss any other relevant subjects that the children would like to find out about. For example, the names of popular children's television and radio programmes, the 'Top Twenty' of the 1950s (or its equivalent), how many television sets and radios people had, where they kept them, how they found out what programmes were going to be on and how people in the family chose what to watch.

✦ Ask them to use different sources for information, such as books about television, radio and listening to music in the past; newspapers; magazine advertisements from the time and also people who remember the 1950s.

 ## Follow-up ideas for history

✦ Ask the children to think of questions that can be answered by someone who remembers the 1950s. Invite someone who lived through the 1950s to come in and answer their questions. The children could write a report of the interview. Ask them to include an introduction that explains the general issues that they wanted to investigate. Then discuss answers that confirmed ideas they already had and answers that surprised them. Conclude with a summary of how helpful the interview was and thank the person whom they interviewed.

✦ Help the children to use old newspapers (available on the Internet, on CD-Roms and in local libraries) to find out about the changes in entertainment over time. Help them to prepare by showing them how to narrow down their searches to avoid wasting time. Ask them to identify the most important changes and find out when they happened and how they came about. Examples include inventions, increases in the amount of money people of different backgrounds had to spare for entertainment, advertising and the availability of goods. The children could place these changes on a class time-line.

These are some of the memories of a person who was born in 1949.

"Wikey, wi – keye!" (Wakey, wakey.) Billy Cotton's voice, introducing 'The Billy Cotton Band Show' every Saturday lunch-time on the Light Programme, is the voice I best remember from the 1950s. My brother and I had to keep absolutely silent, and preferably completely motionless (apart from eating) until it finished. The Light Programme was the BBC's light entertainment radio channel. People called the radio the 'wireless', a term which expressed the idea of the magic of sounds being transmitted from one place to another without any wires connecting those places.

The wireless was a wooden box about the size of a computer monitor, with a speaker behind six or seven ornately-shaped curved slashes in the front of the box, lined with a coarse brown fabric. My parents eventually bought a radiogram – an even bigger wooden box with spindly black legs screwed into its base, making it a free-standing, but rather wobbly, piece of furniture. At one end of it was the radio (it became old-fashioned to call it a 'wireless') and beside that was a lid which opened to reveal a turntable on which gramophone records could be played. The records measured about 30 centimetres across and were made of a hard, very brittle, black shiny plastic material. I remember dropping 'Island in the Sun' by Harry Belafonte onto the linoleum floor. It broke in two. Later, on 'Blue Peter', I learned that you could make things like fruit bowls from unwanted 78 records by softening them in hot water and bending them into shape. (78 meant 78 revolutions per minute – the speed at which you had to play the records.) Later, in the 1960s, we would have an even more modern piece of equipment – a portable record-player which could play records at different speeds; it was great fun playing the 33 and 45 records at 78rpm.

Even after my parents bought a television (the first in our road) in 1956, there were few programmes to watch before late afternoon, except for sports programmes at the weekend. The television set was a huge, dark wooden cabinet, about one and a half metres high and

nearly a metre deep, with a tiny screen and an enormous black metal bump protruding from the back of it (my mother called the bump the 'tube'). The picture was black and white. On the front of the set was a round knob, optimistically numbered from 1 to 10, but there was only one channel – BBC. Sometimes the screen would go blank. "A valve's gone," my father would pronounce, or, even worse, "The tube's gone." By then we had forgotten what we used to do in the evenings before we had a television.

✦ 1 9 5 0 s ' entertainment ✦

✦ Complete the chart to show the differences between radio in the 1950s and now.

	1950s	Now
Radio sets (What they looked like)		
The names of the radio channels		
The names of some radio programmes		
The names of entertainers		
How and when people listened to the radio		

✦ What would you like to find out about radio in the 1950s?
   On the lines below, write a question for each topic.

_____

_____

_____

_____

_____

◆ 1950s' entertainment ◆

✦ In the chart below, make notes on what you know about entertainment in the 1950s.

Radio			
Equipment	Channels	Programmes	People

Television			
Equipment	Channels	Programmes	People

Listening to music			
Equipment	Channels	Record companies	Popular songs

On the back of this sheet, write what you would like to find out more about. List the sources you would use, for example older people, diaries, old newspapers, artefacts and advertisements.

✦ 1950s' entitlement ✦

✦ Complete the chart to plan your research into entertainment in the 1950s. Use the box at the bottom of the page to make notes about what you found out.

Choose one type of entertainment.

Type of entertainment from the 1950s (For example, television, radio or listening to music)		
What I know	What I want to find out	The sources I shall use

Notes: What I found out

You need not write sentences. Miss out words like 'the'. Use abbreviations.

Chapter 5

Emigration in the 1950s

Literacy objectives

- To investigate figures of speech from everyday life. (Y5, T2: W12)
- To distinguish between fact and opinion. (Y6, T1: T11)

History objectives

(Unit 13)
- To learn in depth about the changes in one aspect of the British way of life since 1948.
- To investigate the causes of this change.

Resources

- Copies of posters or other advertisements issued by the Canadian government to encourage people to emigrate there.
- Copies of newspaper and other reports about the situation in Britain in the 1950s, in particular about the Suez crisis and its effects on life in Britain. Useful sources include the *Daily Mail Centenary* and *Encyclopaedia Britannica* CD-Roms and websites such as www.bbc.co.uk/history/.
- A map showing the position of the Suez Canal.

Starting point: Whole class

- Show the children the Suez Canal on a map, and explain 'post-Suez' – the period following the Suez crisis, when Britain had joined France and Israel in a military attack to prevent General Nasser from nationalising the Suez Canal (in Egypt) in 1956. Explain that the Suez Canal was an important shipping route and that oil from the Arabian Gulf countries was brought to Britain via the canal. When General Nasser seized control of it, the transport of oil to Britain was restricted. The fuel shortage worsened when allies such as the USA banned the export of oil and other goods to Britain in protest at Britain's part in the Suez attack. Petrol was rationed and heavily taxed (one shilling [5p] per gallon). The budgets of 1955–1957 imposed high taxes which discouraged spending and made most people worse off financially than they had been. The tax on fuel made everything more expensive because of increased transport costs.
- Explain that Richard Austen (RAB) Butler was Chancellor of the Exchequer in 1951 (and Lord Privy Seal and then Leader of the House of Commons in 1955). He stepped in as deputy when prime minister

Anthony Eden resigned through ill health just after the Suez crisis. Harold Macmillan was Chancellor from 1955 to 1957 and became Prime Minister after that.
- Show the children the newspaper reports about the events and then show them the advertisements which invited people in Britain to emigrate to Canada in the mid to late 1950s. Can they explain why people might have wanted to emigrate?

Using the photocopiable text

- Enlarge the text on page 30 or make a copy for each child. Share the text with the children.
- Discuss what the text is about. Discuss the jobs described in the report. Explain that a stenographer was someone who could write in shorthand. Explain what shorthand is and how it was used by typists who would take notes of letters or other documents dictated to them. Ask the children if they know of anyone who is a stenographer. Tell them there are few stenographers or typists today. Can they explain why?
- Discuss the purposes of newspaper reports (to tell people the facts, to influence their opinions, to influence the government). What message is this report giving to the people and to the government of the day?
- Underline some figures of speech or idiomatic phrases in the text, for example 'John Bull Taxpayer', 'Macmillan Squeeze Budget' and 'belt-tightening'. What do the children think they mean? Use dictionaries (such as *Brewer's Dictionary of Phrase and Fable*) to find out.
- Revise the meanings of the words 'fact' and 'opinion' and ask the children what facts they can find in the newspaper report. What opinions can they find? Discuss the ways in which they can recognise explicit opinions (introduced with phrases such as 'I think', 'My view is' or 'Surely most people would agree') and implicit opinions, which are more difficult to spot, since they might be presented as if they are facts, such as 'He is the type of man Britain cannot afford to lose.'

Group activities

Activity sheet 1: This is for children who are beginning to distinguish fact from opinion. They need help in identifying the facts and opinions within a text.

Activity sheet 2: This is for children who know the difference between fact and opinion and, with the help of a structured table, can identify facts and explicit opinions in a text.

Emigration in the 1950s

Activity sheet 3: This is for children who can distinguish between fact and opinion in a text. They can identify implicit as well as explicit opinions and can comment on the different effects of a purely factual text and one in which opinions are expressed.

Plenary session

+ Begin with Activity sheet 1 and invite the children to share their responses. Ask them how they could tell whether the sentences gave a fact or an opinion. The first example is expressed as if it were a fact. How can they tell that it is an opinion? Question them about the meaning of the sentence. People have had enough of what? Which people? How could the writer know? Can it be verified? Compare this with the sentence 'Two men in every three own their own homes.' How can they tell that this is a fact? (It can be verified.)

+ Move on to Activity sheet 2 and ask the children to justify some of their responses in the same way.

+ Invite one of the children who completed Activity sheet 3 to read out their altered report. The others could check that no opinions have been left in it and comment on the difference made by removing them.

Follow-up ideas for literacy

+ The children could investigate idiomatic phrases and figures of speech in present-day newspaper articles and others from the 1950s and comment on how everyday language has changed. They could rewrite passages, replacing the idiomatic phrases and figures of speech with plainer language, and comment on the effects of the changes. They could also try using these expressions in their own writing.

+ Discuss events which are currently in the news and ask the children to read newspaper reports, looking for facts and both explicit and implicit opinions. They could make charts on which to list them.

Follow-up ideas for history

+ Discuss the attitudes shown in the passage towards men and women. What do the children notice about the wages of skilled men and women, and about the view of the relative importance of women's and men's work? Point out that, for married couples, the man was considered to be the home-owner, and not the woman. The children might also notice that women were expected to be interested in running a home. The family car was considered to be the husband's concern. Explain that few families had more than one car (if any) in the 1950s and that few women could drive. The children could use other sources from the time to research the different attitudes towards, and the different rights of, men and women.

+ Using local directories, the children could find out about people from their own localities. For example, what work did they do, and how has employment changed since the 1950s? They could find out about a family who emigrated to Canada in the 1950s, for example how they travelled there, what work they did in Britain and then in Canada and whether their wages and standard of living changed after emigrating.

Daily Mail   An investigation by RHONA CHURCHILL   **8 January 1957**

WHILE Mr. Macmillan prepares his post-Suez Budget, John Bull Taxpayer plans his escape. Emigrant applications at Canada's London and Liverpool offices have now reached 20,000 a week.

John Bull Taxpayer has had enough.

Emigration figures had been falling off. Then suddenly the Butler Austerity Budget of October 1955 doubled the numbers calling at Canadian immigration offices, the Macmillan Squeeze Budget of April 1956 trebled them, and Suez, with its promise of still more Budget austerity, increased them sixfold.

An escape

A QUARTER OF A MILLION Britons, tired of being told for ten austere years: "Belt-tightening today means prosperity tomorrow," and, finding that tomorrow never comes, are now organising their escape, believing that Britain has no sound financial future to offer their children. At least 500,000 more are thinking of making inquiries.

What sort of man is this 1957 emigrant? A loafer? An adventurer? By no means. He is a skilled artisan earning good union rates. He is the type of man Britain cannot afford to lose.

He is a man like John Sykes, a 49-year-old aircraft factory draughtsman, with a wife, aged 47, three children, a weekly wage of £11 10s. and yearly savings of £12. Or Douglas Young, a 24-year-old printer, wife, two children, £11 6s. a week, savings of £10 a year. These men, chosen from thousands queuing at Canada's London immigration office in Green Street, are typical.

Why Canada?

WHY have they picked Canada as their land of promise? What can they expect from life in this expanding and potentially wealthy Dominion?

To begin with, each man will more than double his salary the day he lands in Canada. His cost of living will rise 50 per cent at most.

Two men in every three own their own homes. If John Emigrant turns out to be only an average fellow he will earn £24 a week, save £125 a year and, with two children, pay only £1 a week income tax. In Britain the same average chap earns £11 15s. 4d a week and saves £12 4s. 9d a year. His tax on £24 a week would be more than £3 a week. Skilled artisans earn more. John Sykes will start at £25 and rise quickly to £30. Douglas Young will start at £28.

If their wives want to help at first by taking jobs as stenographers they will easily earn £15 a week.

John Emigrant, if he is the type of worker Canada wants, and sound in mind and lung, can borrow his own and his family's fare from the Canadian Government on a two-year repayment basis. This shows how certain Canada is that he will settle down and make good.

He need not have a job to go to. As an artisan he will get one for the asking. Professional men are being advised to take £500 to tide them over the first weeks while they search for their ideal job. But inexperienced young architects can quickly land jobs paying £1,600 a year. Chemists can wave the Welfare State good-bye and open shops in Canada within six months of settling.

Cosy home

AND Mrs John Emigrant? What of her, leaving her semi-detached three-bedroomed council house? She should soon be running a streamlined home centrally heated by cheap oil, with a thermostat set to maintain the temperature at 70 degrees.

Among her first household purchases will be an enormous refrigerator and a fully automatic washing machine.

Her husband will soon be making the down-payment on a Rolls-sized limousine, bought for less than a small car in England.

He can afford it. He will only be living like his neighbours, warmly, cosily, even plushly by the standards of the people he has left behind.

✦ Fact or opinion? ✦

✦ Which sentences give facts and which express opinions?
   Mark them F (fact) or O (opinion).

People have had enough. ☐	They believe that Britain offers no sound future for their children. ☐	Each man will more than double his salary when he arrives in Canada. ☐
If he turns out to be an average fellow he will earn £24 per week. ☐	This shows how certain Canada is that he will settle down and make good. ☐	He can be accepted as an immigrant without having a job to do. ☐
He will find work almost as soon as he arrives in Canada. ☐	She should soon be running a streamlined home. ☐	Skilled artisans earn more than unskilled workers. ☐
20,000 people are applying to emigrate to Canada each week. ☐	Two men in every three own their own homes. ☐	He will be living in luxury in comparison with people in Britain. ☐
A quarter of a million Britons are tired of being told "Belt-tightening today means prosperity tomorrow." ☐	Canada is in the north of the continent of North America. ☐	Canada is likely to become a wealthy dominion. ☐

✦ Look for another fact and another opinion in the newspaper report.

Fact _____

Opinion _____

Name _____

✦ Fact or opinion? ✦

✦ List any facts and opinions you can find in the newspaper report.

Write as briefly as you can.

Facts	Opinions
There were now 20,000 applications per week for emigration to Canada.	

✦ Underline any opinions which are expressed as if they were facts.

Activity 3

Name _____

✦Fact or opinion?✦

✦ Rewrite the newspaper report, giving only the facts.

Mr Macmillan is preparing his post-Suez budget. Emigrant applications at Canada's London and Liverpool offices have now reached 20,000 per week. _____

_____

_____

_____

_____

_____

_____

_____

_____

_____

_____

Think about the purposes of newspaper reports. Are newspapers biased? What is this article saying to people about the government? What is it saying to the government?

_____

_____

_____

✦ What differences did your changes make?

Continue on the back of this page or on another sheet of paper.

33

©Hopscotch Educational Publishing

The gods and goddesses of Ancient Greece

 Literacy objectives

+ To develop the skills of biographical and autobiographical writing in role, adopting distinctive voices for example, of historical characters through preparing a CV. (Y6, T1: T14)

 History objectives

(Unit 14)
+ To learn about the beliefs of the Ancient Greeks.

 Resources

+ Maps of Greece and Athens.
+ Pictures of the Acropolis and other temples.
+ Pictures and copies of statues of Greek gods and goddesses.
+ Books about Ancient Greek gods and goddesses.

Note: There are different versions of some of the Greek legends.

 Starting point: Whole class

+ Talk about how we know about the beliefs of the Ancient Greeks, for example from plays, epic poems, pictures and artefacts such as temples, statues and vases.
+ Show the children a map of Greece and help them to locate Mount Olympus. Explain that it was the legendary home of the gods. Ask the children to summarise any stories they have read about the Greek gods.
+ Display a picture of the Acropolis. Help the children to locate it on a map of Athens and to find Athens on a map of Greece. Have any of the children been to Athens or any other part of Greece? If so, they could talk about any temples they saw. Ensure that they do not assume that modern Greeks worship the gods to whom the temples were dedicated.
+ Show them pictures (for example, from statues, friezes and vases) of the Ancient Greek gods and goddesses. Ask the children what they can deduce about the deities from the pictures.

 Using the photocopiable text

+ Enlarge the text on page 36 or make a copy for each child. Explain that the type of text from which it is taken is not meant to be read from beginning to end, but to be used for finding out specific types of information about the gods. Discuss any unfamiliar vocabulary such as 'mortal' and 'immortal'.
+ Ask the children to use the chart to answer questions, for example:
  – Who was the god of war?
  – Which god could make thunderbolts?
  – Which goddesses took part in the Judgement of Paris?
  – Which goddess won the contest for the golden apple of Paris?
  – Of what was Hestia the goddess?
  – Whom did Artemis turn into a bear?
  – For which land did Athena and Poseidon compete?
+ The children could also think of questions for the others to answer, using the chart.
+ Do they know any information (from legends they have read or from the introductory discussion) that could be added to the chart?
+ Explain the meaning of 'curriculum vitae' and about its derivation (from the Latin words which mean 'course' and 'of life'). Say that 'CV' is the usual abbreviation for 'curriculum vitae' and explain what a CV is for.
+ Tell the children that they are going to write a CV. Model this for one of the gods on the chart on page 36. Together, research more information about one of them and write their CV on the board. (You could use the information about Hermes on Activity sheet 1. This will help prepare the children who will be doing this activity sheet independently.) Explain that the shorter sections of a CV need not be filled in with complete sentences. For example, on Activity sheet 2, for parents they can write 'Zeus and Metis' and for 'Special features of birth', they could write 'Sprang from the forehead of Zeus when Hephaistos cut it open with an axe.'

 Group activities

Activity sheet 1: This is for children who can locate information in a short text and are learning to present this information in different forms. They benefit from the support of a ready-made structure for their writing.

Activity sheet 2: This is for children who can scan a text to find the information they need, decide if it is useful and organise this information on a chart.

Literacy through history

The gods and goddesses of Ancient Greece

Activity sheet 3: This is for children who can scan different sources to find specific information. They can organise information from different sources in a coherent way and use it for a specific purpose.

Plenary session

✦ Begin with Activity sheets 1 and 2. Invite the children to share their responses. If their responses differ, discuss these differences and resolve any errors or omissions.

Move on to Activity sheet 3 and ask the children which god or goddess they chose, what they could find out from the chart and what other information they found from a book. Did they leave any sections of the CV blank? Can the others supply the missing information, or is it not known? Invite some of the children to read out the CVs they wrote for one of the gods.

Follow up ideas for literacy

✦ Invite the children to re-write the story of one of the Greek deities in the form of a playscript, and enact it in their group. Show them, or revise, the layout of playscripts and ask them to include a description of the set, stage directions and the characters' names to the left of the words they speak. Compare the different layout of speech in a play and a story.

✦ Read Greek legends with the children and help them to identify the key characteristics of the genre, for example love, punishment, revenge and struggles for power. Compare Greek legends with legends from other cultures and identify similarities and differences. Organise their responses on a chart.

Legend	Culture	Characteristics			
		Love	Punishment	Revenge	Power struggles

Follow up ideas for history

✦ Help the children to use a range of sources (pictures, information books, electronic texts, legends, poems and pictures) to find out more about specific gods and goddesses. Let them scan the chart on page 36 into the computer and add to it. For example, they could add other deities, another column (such as 'family' or 'symbols') and further information.

✦ The children could use different sources to find out how and where the Greeks worshipped. For example, they could research the use of sacrifices, prayers, hymns or songs and how the Greeks worshipped in temples, at home or outdoors. Ask them to find out how the beliefs of the Ancient Greeks affected their everyday life (for example, their belief in prophecy and their consultations with the oracle).

Literacy through history

35

Name	Role	History	Features and talents
Aphrodite	Goddess of love	Along with Athena and Hera, claimed the golden apple thrown down by Paris. He asked them to make an offer for it. She offered the loveliest woman as his wife. Won. Helped him to win Helen of Troy as his bride.	Beauty
Apollo	God of music, poetry, nature, phrophecy, archery.	Son of Zeus. Saved Delphi by killing the dragon Python (guardian of the oracle) and made it his home.	Playing the lyre
Ares	God of war	Defeated by mortals: imprisoned in a bronze jar for thirteen months by two mortal giants.	Stirring up strife
Artemis	Goddess of the Moon, wildlife	Daughter of Zeus and twin sister of Apollo. Turned Callisto into a bear.	Forever a virgin
Athena	Patron goddess of Athens	Birth: sprang from forehead of Zeus. Won land of Attica by giving inhabitants an olive tree, defeating Poseidon (who gave a horse). In the golden apple contest, offered Paris success in war.	Beauty
Demeter	Goddess of corn, agriculture	Her daughter, Persephone, was taken by Hades to underworld (caused winter). Persephone allowed out of underworld for half the year to bring summer.	Could make mortals immortal
Dionysus	God of wine	Son of Zeus. Persecuted by those who did not believe he was immortal (including the daughters of Proteus, whom he drove mad, making them kill their daughters).	Turning himself into a wild animal (for example, lion) when in danger
Hephaestus	God of fire, blacksmiths	Hera threw him out of heaven because he was lame. In revenge sent her a golden chair which locked her in once she sat on it.	Metalwork, making thunderbolts
Hera	Queen of heaven, goddess of women	In golden apple contest judged by Paris, offered him world-wide rule.	Stateliness and beauty
Hestia	Goddess of hearth, home, family	Hearth in every home consecrated to her. Sacred fire to her on Olympus and at Delphi. Mentioned in all prayers.	Forever a virgin
Poseidon	God of sea, earthquakes	Defeated by Athena for land of Attica. Tried to kill Odysseus to punish him for blinding Polyphemus.	Violence, bad temper
Zeus	King of heaven, sky, weather	Cast lots with his brothers, Hades and Poseidon, to share out the universe. He got heaven, Poseidon the sea and Hades the underworld.	Power of dispensing good and evil, prophecy

◆ A curriculum vitae for Hermes ◆

✦ Read this information about Hermes.

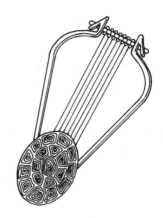

Hermes was very clever. He was the ancient Greek god of luck, wealth, thieves and merchants. He was also the messenger of the gods.

On the day he was born he killed a tortoise and made a lyre from its shell. He then drove off 50 cows that belonged to the god Apollo, making them walk backwards so that they could not be traced.

✦ See what else you can find out about Hermes. Complete as much of his curriculum vitae as you can.

Curriculum vitae	
Name	Parents
Status (mortal or immortal)	
Address	Special features of birth
Skills	Talents
Additional information	

A curriculum vitae for Athena

◆ Read this story of Athena and then fill in her curriculum vitae.

Athena was the daughter of Zeus and Metis. Hephaestus cut open the forehead of Zeus with an axe and out sprang Athena.

Zeus made Athena responsible for the planning of warfare. She fought alongside the Greeks against the Trojans and inspired many of their victories.

Athena and Poseidon both wanted to win the land of Attica. The gods asked them what they would give to the people there. Athena offered an olive tree. Poseidon offered a horse. The gods decided Athena's gift was more useful. She became the patron of Athens and of all cities.

Athena invented the flute and became the patron of the arts and handicrafts and the goddess of wisdom. A great temple, the Parthenon, was built in her honour on the hill known as the Acropolis in Athens.

Curriculum vitae	
Name	Parents
Status (mortal or immortal) Proof	
Address	Special features of birth
Skills	Talents
Notable achievements	Patronage (places, groups of people, activities)
Special honours received	

©Hopscotch Educational Publishing

◆ A CV for a god or goddess ◆

◆ Scan a book about Greek myths and legends to find out about one of the Greek gods or goddesses. Complete the CV below for him or her.

Curriculum Vitae	
Name	Parents
Status (mortal or immortal) Proof	
Address	Special features of birth
God/Goddess of (state all areas of responsibility)	Animals and other symbols (state all)
Skills	Talents and magic powers (if any)
Notable achievements	Patronage (places, groups of people, activities)
Special honours received (statues, buildings, dedications)	
Stories, myths and poems in which I am featured	

Ancient Greek writing

 ## Literacy objectives

- To identify words from other languages. (Y5, T3: W8)
- To use prefixes as a support for spelling. (Y5, T1: W6; Y6: T1, W5)
- To use dictionaries efficiently to explore derivations. (Y5, T3: W12)

 ## History objectives

(Unit 15)

- To learn about the language and written alphabet of the ancient Greeks.
- To recognise similarities and differences between the Greek and English alphabets.

 ## Resources

- Holiday brochures and postcards of Greece.
- Pictures of Greek inscriptions on buildings, statues, coins and other artefacts.
- Dictionaries (printed and electronic) which include the derivations of words (for example, *The Shorter Oxford Dictionary*) and etymological dictionaries.

 ## Starting Point: Whole class

- Before the lesson, ask if any of the children have been to Greece and if so what they visited there and what they liked about the country. Ask them to bring in artefacts, pictures, postcards, brochures, maps and coins connected with Greece.
- Invite the children to look closely at any writing on the items (including the stamps on postcards). Can they read it? Find any words they cannot read and discuss what makes reading them so difficult.
- Tell the children that the term 'Ancient Greece' refers to the time from about 1200–200BCE (Before the Common Era). Explain that the Ancient Greeks had a written language that used the same alphabet as that of the modern Greek language. Show the children pictures of Ancient Greek artefacts on which there are inscriptions. They could copy some of the words from the inscriptions (to be read later, once they have seen the Greek alphabet).

Using the photocopiable text

- Make an enlarged copy of the two tables on page 42 and display them. Alternatively, make enough copies for each child (or pair) to have a copy.
- Ask the children to look up the meanings of 'history', 'technology' and 'geography' in a dictionary. What do they notice about the derivations of the words? Invite them to look up the names of other subjects and record any that are derived from Greek. Encourage them to split the words into segments. Can they think of any other words that contain some of the same segments, for example 'geography/geology/geometry' and 'technology/technical'?
- Look at the letters of the Greek alphabet and compare them with the letters from today's English alphabet.
- Cover the English words and the pictures. Can the children read any of the Greek words, with the help of the alphabet? Help them to transliterate the first word; if necessary reveal the picture as a clue, and then uncover the English word. (Note that the matches of Greek and English words are not exact. However, if the children look up the English words in an etymological dictionary they will find the Greek derivation. So the derivation of 'tiger' is 'tigris' and of 'orchid' is 'orchis'.) Repeat this process for the names of the other plants and animals.
- Introduce (or revise) the term 'prefix' and discuss its meaning. Show the children examples of words to which prefixes can be added (for example 'national/international', 'tone/monotone' and 'cycle/bicycle'). They should notice that adding a prefix changes the meaning but not the spelling of a word. Explain that many prefixes in English come from Greek. Invite the children to look up a few examples of words with prefixes in the dictionary and find their derivations.

Group activities

Activity sheet 1: This is for children who are learning to identify prefixes. They know that a prefix is added to the beginning of a root word and that the meaning of a prefix remains the same when it is added to different words. They are beginning to build up a vocabulary of prefixes.

Activity sheet 2: This is for children who can identify prefixes. They can work out the meanings of words beginning with known prefixes, and are beginning to recognise links between words with common prefixes (and common roots).

Activity sheet 3: This is for children who know that a prefix is added to the beginning of a root word and that

Literacy through history

KS2: Y5–6

Ancient Greek writing

the meaning of a prefix remains the same when it is added to different words. They can identify the correct prefix to convey a specific meaning and have the necessary vocabulary to infer the correct word.

Plenary session

+ Invite the children who completed Activity sheet 1 to give the meanings of some of the prefixes (without looking at the activity sheet). You could also ask them to 'give the prefix which means …'. Encourage them to share their responses to the activity, and discuss the meanings of the root words to which the prefixes were

added. For example, look at the root word 'graph', and ask which words contain this root.

+ Move on to Activity sheet 2 and invite the children to read out their responses. Ask them if they can tell to which class of word each one on the list belongs, for example a noun, verb, adjective and so on. Ask them to check that they have used the words correctly in the sentences they wrote. Can they see any words containing the same roots to which different prefixes can be added, for example 'telescope' and 'microscope'?

+ The children who completed Activity sheet 3 could explain how they worked out the right words for the meanings listed.

Follow-up ideas for literacy

+ Begin a class database of words derived from Greek to which the children can contribute as they come across them.

The database could be organised as a table which arranges the words in alphabetical order so that new words can be added at any time.

English word	Greek derivation	Meaning	Links with other words
abacus	*abakos, abax* (slab)	counting frame	
autograph	*autographos* (written with one's own hand)	a person's signature	automatic, autogyro
dinosaur	*deinos* (fearsome, terrible) *sauros* (lizard)	an extinct reptile	stegosaurus, brontosaurus
dynamo	*dunamis* (force)	a machine that converts energy from movement into electricity	dynamic, dynamite

Follow-up ideas for history

+ The children could transliterate Greek words from inscriptions from different sources (such as information books, electronic texts, posters and pictures of inscriptions on temples and statues). They could use the Internet to look for Greek inscriptions on exhibits from museums, such as the website of the British Museum – www.thebritishmuseum.ac.uk/. Enter 'Ancient Greece' in its search facility to see thumbnails of a collection of artefacts, which can be looked at in detail. Enlarge the images so that you can read the inscriptions.

+ The children could use reference books and electronic texts (such as *Encyclopaedia Britannica* CD-Rom or its website www.Britannica.com) to look up the names of any people or places they recognise on the inscriptions.

Literacy through history

41

The Greek Alphabet			
1	2	3	4
A	α	alpha	ah
B	β	beta	b
Γ	γ	gamma	g
Δ	δ	delta	d
E	ε	epsilon	e
Z	ζ	zeta	sd
H	η	eta	air
Θ	θ	theta	th
I	ι	iota	i
K	κ	kappa	k
Λ	λ	lambda	l
M	μ	mu	m
N	ν	nu	n
Ξ	ξ	xi	x
O	o	omikron	o
Π	π	pi	p
P	ρ	rho	r
Σ	σ ς	sigma*	s
T	τ	tau	t
Y	υ	upsilon	yu
Φ	φ	phi	ph
X	χ	chi	c
Ψ	ψ	psi	ps
Ω	ω	omega	aw

Cat Καττα	Delphinium Δελφινιον	Crocus Κροκος
Iris Ιρις	Eucalyptus Ευκαλυπτος	Orchid Ορχις
Mouse Μυς	Tiger Τιγρις	Panther Πανθηρ
Elephant Ελεφας	Crocodile Κροκοδελος	Rhinoceros Ρινοκερως

Key: 1: upper case letter; 2: lower case letter; 3: name of letter; 4: pronunciation
*Note: Sigma – At the beginning or in the middle of a word σ is used for sigma (s).
At the end of a word ς is used for sigma (s).

◆ Using prefixes ◆

◆ The following prefixes come from the Greek language.

Prefix	Meaning	Prefix	Meaning	Prefix	Meaning
auto	self	deca	ten	kilo	thousand
micro	small	mono	alone	penta	five
photo	light	poly	many	tele	far

◆ Underline the prefixes in the words in the lists below.

autobiography	kilometre	monologue	polygon
automobile	microphone	pentagon	polyhedron
decagon	microscope	pentathlon	telephone
decathlon	monochrome	photograph	telescope

◆ Now choose the correct words from the list above and write them next to their meanings below. Cross out the words in the list as you choose them.

1. A distance of one thousand metres_____

2. An instrument for looking at very small things_____

3. An instrument for looking at things which are far away _____

4. A person's life story written by himself or herself _____

5. A five-sided plane shape _____

6. A sporting competition of ten events_____

7. A solid form with many faces _____

8. An instrument for making sounds louder _____

9. A plane shape with many sides _____

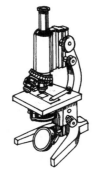

◆ Choose three of the words from the list above that you have not crossed out. Use a dictionary to find their meanings and what their Greek prefixes are. Write these on the back of this sheet.

Activity 2

✦ Using prefixes ✦

✦ The following prefixes come from the Greek language.

Prefix	Meaning	Prefix	Meaning	Prefix	Meaning
auto	self	deca	ten	kilo	thousand
micro	small	mono	alone	penta	five
photo	light	poly	many	tele	far

✦ Underline the prefixes in the words in the list below. Then use a dictionary to find the meanings of the words and write the meanings in your own words alongside them.

1. autobiography _____
2. automobile _____
3. decagon _____
4. decathlon _____
5. kilometre _____
6. microphone _____
7. microscope _____
8. monochrome _____
9. monologue _____
10. pentagon _____
11. pentathlon _____
12. photograph _____
13. polygon _____
14. polyhedron _____
15. telephone _____
16. telescope _____

✦ On the back of this sheet write sentences using three of the words.

✦ Using prefixes ✦

✦ The following prefixes come from the Greek language.

Prefix	Meaning	Prefix	Meaning	Prefix	Meaning
auto	self	deca	ten	kilo	thousand
micro	small	mono	alone	penta	five
photo	light	poly	many	tele	far

✦ Write the words that you think have the following meanings.
Use a dictionary to check them.

1.   A mass of one thousand grams _____

2.   A photographic film on which very small images are recorded _____

3.   An instrument for looking at things that are far away _____

4.   A five-pointed star _____

5.   A person's own signature _____

6.   A period of ten years _____

7.   A solid form with five faces _____

8.   A vehicle with an engine (self-moving) _____

9.   A train running on one rail _____

10.   The process through which plants make their food using light _____

11.   A very tiny living thing (often called a germ) _____

12.   A plane shape with many sides _____

13.   A speech given by one person _____

✦ Choose five of the words you have found. Write a sentence using each of them.

✦ Find other words which use each of the prefixes in the chart above.
Write them on the back of this sheet.

The Roanoke settlement

 Literacy objectives

- To write a recount based on an historical event. (Y5, T1: T24)
- To use the styles and conventions of journalism to report on events. (Y6, T1: T16)
- To understand how words and expressions have changed over time. (Y6, T1: W7)

 History objectives

(Unit 19)

- To apply knowledge and understanding of settlement in England to a new context – settlement in America.
- To understand the difficulties which faced the settlers in Roanoke.

 Resources

- A map of the USA showing the location of North Carolina.
- A map showing the position of Roanoke and the Fort Raleigh visitor centre.
- Copies of John White's drawings of the indigenous people of Roanoke.
- Pictures of the English ships that sailed to Roanoke, of the settlement and the settlers.
- Some copies of present-day daily newspapers.

 Starting point: Whole class

- Ask the children what they know about people who settled in America in the past and why they left their own countries. Discuss what it might have been like to leave their homes to make a sea voyage – which could take months – to an unknown land. How did people travel in the past? Compare this with present-day travel.
- Show them a map of America and the position of North Carolina, then a map showing the position of Roanoke. Explain that in 1585 Sir Walter Raleigh had been granted a patent by Queen Elizabeth of England to set up a colony in America. He had led the first expedition to Roanoke in 1587 and about 100 English people had now settled there. Discuss the kinds of preparations that people would have had to make for this voyage, and for their survival when they arrived. What would they have done once their supplies of food had been used up and when they needed clothing and other items?

- Remind the children that other people already inhabited this land. How might they have reacted to the newcomers? Discuss the possibility of hostility and the opportunities for trade on both sides. Show the children some pictures of the Roanoke settlement and ask them what they tell us about the event.
- Explain that, to begin with, the indigenous Secotan people had welcomed the visitors, traded with them, given them food and agreed to supply them with corn. Ralph Lane, governor of the colony, had returned to England for supplies but, before he left, relations with the Secotan had become strained. This was partly because the demands made on the local food supply were too great and because the English had held some of the Secotans hostage in exchange for information about gold mines they thought existed in the area.

 Using the photocopiable text

- Tell the children that they are going to share a passage from a recount written at the time. Explain that John White's job during the expeditions to Roanoke was to record information about the land and its people. He was also an artist who drew and painted pictures of the land, the settlement and the people.
- Make a copy of the text on page 48 for each child and read it with them. What do they notice about the layout? (It is not split into paragraphs.) During the initial reading do not stop at any difficult words.
- Invite the children to retell the passage, so that you are able to identify how much of it they understood. Ask them to point out any words they did not understand. 'Cortynes' probably meant curtain walls (defensive walls); 'flankers' were fortifications on the flank of a building; a 'Pinnisse' (pinnace) was a light ship (usually two-masted) which was used mainly for sailing between the commander's ship and the rest of the fleet; 'Iron sacker-shotte' was a kind of ammunition for cannons.
- The children could also identify words they can understand but whose spellings are different from their modern spellings. List these words with their modern spellings. Discuss the use of capital letters in the report. The children could identify words in the passage which would not need initial capital letters in modern spelling.
- Point out any words that have become obsolete, for example 'sithence' (since), and give their modern equivalents. Look for phrases and sentence structures with archaic forms and unconventional tense-formations (for example, 'digged').
- Tell the children that they are going to use the information in the text to write a newspaper report.

Literacy through history

The Roanoke settlement

Look at some newspaper stories to familiarise the children with the written style and format. Point out the key features: the headline and subheading for gaining the attention of readers; an opening sentence to help the reader know what the report is about; the use of illustrations; the use of connectives; the level of formality (it is an impersonal style of writing – there is usually no use of 'I', 'me' or 'you'). Remind the children that the past tense is used for a recount (although headlines and subheadings can be in the present tense, and need not be complete sentences).

 ## Group activities

Activity sheet 1: This is for children who need the support of cloze procedure for writing simple recounts.

Activity sheet 2: This is for children who can write simple recounts but need help in structuring more complex ones. They can recognise some features of journalistic writing and, with support, can write in a journalistic style.

Activity sheet 3: This is for children who can write recounts competently, in a way that engages and retains the interest of their audience. They have a good understanding of the journalistic style of writing and can use it confidently in writing recounts.

 ## Plenary session

◆ Invite the children to read from their work. The others could comment on any sentences or phrases which engage and keep their interest. Discuss the ending of their recount. Does it offer some ideas as to what became of the settlers at Roanoke? Would it encourage readers to buy the newspaper again to find out more?

◆ Notice how well the children maintained an impersonal style, kept to the past tense consistently (except for any speculation at the end), kept to the correct chronological sequence and used connectives. How well did they manage to avoid the repetition of '…then'?

 ## Follow-up ideas for literacy

◆ The children could compile a class glossary of Tudor language to help them to understand other documents from the time. They could order it alphabetically themselves or use a table on a word-processor.

◆ Using the photocopiable text and other texts from this period, the children could collect examples of the formations of tenses that differ from modern English.

◆ The children could write a continuation of the story which recounts the adventures of the colonists whom John White and his company could not find, including how they felt when the supply ship failed to find them, how they found food, their relationship with the local Secotan people, and what became of the settlers in the end.

 ## Follow-up ideas for history

◆ The children could research the Roanoke settlement using information books and websites. A useful website, run by the National Park Service of the USA at Fort Raleigh historical centre on Roanoke, www.nps.gov/fora/, gives the names of some of the Native Americans who traded with, and helped, the English settlers, as well as accounts of the voyages of Sir Walter Raleigh and others to Roanoke. The children can read governor Ralph Lane's account of the colony (written in 1586) on the American

Colonists' Library website: www.nationalcenter.org/ColonyofRoanoke.html.

◆ The children could use these websites and the websites of museums in Britain, as well as information books, to find out about the way of life of the indigenous people of Roanoke. Tell them that we know about these people from the records made by John White, Thomas Hariot and other English chroniclers who went to Roanoke.

'Return To Roanoke' by John White (1590) from *Principal Navigations, Voyages of the English Nation III* (Richard Hakluyt, 1600).

We came to the place where I left our Colony in the yeere 1586. In all this way we saw in the sand the print of the Savages feet troaden yt night, and as we entred up the sandy banke, upon a tree, in the very browe thereof were curiously carved these faire Romane letters C R O: which letters presently we knew to signifie the place where I should find the planters seated, according to a secret token agreed upon betweene them & me at my last departure from them. At my departure from them in Anno 1587 I willed them, that if they should happen to be distressed, that then they should carve over the letters or name, a Crosse in this forme, but we found no such signe of distresse. And having well considered of this, we passed toward the place where they were left in sundry houses, but we found the houses taken downe, and the place very strongly enclosed with a high palisado of great trees, with cortynes and flankers very Fort-like. We entred into the palisado, where we found many barres of Iron, two pigges of Lead, foure yron fowlers, Iron sacker-shotte, and such like heavie things, throwen here and there, almost overgrowen with grasse and weedes. From thence wee went along by the water side, towards the poynt of the Creeke to see if we could find any of their botes or Pinnisse, but we could perceive no signe of them. At our returne from the Creeke, some of our Saylers meeting us, tolde us that they had found where chests had bene hidden, and long sithence digged up againe and broken up, and much of the goods in them spoyled and scattered about, but nothing left, of such things as the Savages knew any use of, undefaced. Presently Captaine Cooke and I went to the place, which was in the ende of an olde trench, made two yeeres past by Captaine Amadas: wheere wee found five Chests, that had been carefully hidden of the Planters, and of the same chests three were my owne, and about the place many of my things spoyled and broken, and my bookes torne from the covers, the frames of some of my pictures and Mappes rotten and spoyled with rayne, and my armour almost eaten through with rust; this could bee no other but the deede of the Savages our enemies at Dasamongwepeuk, who had watched the departure of our men to Croatoan; and as soone as they were departed, digged up every place where they suspected any thing to be buried: but although it much grieved me to see such spoyle of my goods, yet on the other side I greatly joyed that I had safely found a certaine token of their safe being at Croatoan, which is the place where Manteo* was borne, and the Savages of the Iland our friends. When we had seene in this place so much as we could, we returned to our Boates, and departed from the shoare towards our Shippes, with as much speede as we could.

*Manteo was a Secotan who went to England with one of the first expeditions to return from Roanoke. He and another of his people agreed to teach the English about their language and way of life. (A storm prevented the ships from sailing to Croatoan. The 90 men, 17 women and nine children who had settled at Roanoke were never seen again.)

✦ A newspaper report ✦

✦ Complete the report for an English newspaper about the expedition to Roanoke.
   Remember to write in the past tense.

Headline	**NO SIGN OF SETTLERS** **ROANOKE DESERTED** **MYSTERY IN ROANOKE** John White reports from Roanoke
Subheading	*Lane's ships return safely* *Savages destroy settlement* *Settlement plundered by natives*

> Underline the headline and subheading you like best. Or write your own. Headlines and subheadings need not be complete sentences. They can be in the present tense.

Recount

No settlers came to meet our ships when we landed at _____.
The only prints in the sand were the bare _____ of the _____.

On a _____ we _____ the letters _____. These three letters told me where I would _____ the _____. There was no _____ over the _____. This told us that all was well with them.

When we _____ at the place where the _____ were, we found they had been taken _____ and the place enclosed with a palisado of _____ making it like a _____.

We found our chests but they had been _____ up and the contents

Picture

Caption

_____

were _____ about. My _____ were torn and my _____ eaten with _____.

Who could have carried out this wanton destruction but the _____?

We left this _____ and departed for our ships with as much _____ as we could.

49

◆ A newspaper report ◆

◆ Complete the report for an English newspaper about the expedition to Roanoke.
Continue on the back of the sheet if necessary. Remember to write in the past tense.

Headline	**NO SIGN OF SETTLERS** **ROANOKE DESERTED** **MYSTERY IN ROANOKE** John White reports from Roanoke

> Underline the headline and subheading you like best. Or write your own. Headlines and subheadings need not be complete sentences. They can be in the present tense.

Subheading	*Lane's ships return safely* *Savages destroy settlement* *Settlement plundered by natives*

Recount

No settlers came to meet our ships when we landed at Roanoke. The only prints in the sand were the bare footprints of the natives.

On a tree we found

These three letters told me

The absence of a cross over the letters told us

Where there were once settlers' houses we found

Our buried chests of valuables

Who could have carried out this wanton destruction but the natives?

Picture

Caption

_____

◆ A newspaper report ◆

◆ Complete the report for an English newspaper about the expedition to Roanoke.
Write in the past tense. Continue on the back of the sheet if necessary.

Headline	**NO SIGN OF SETTLERS** **ROANOKE DESERTED** **MYSTERY IN ROANOKE** John White reports from Roanoke

Underline the headline and subheading you like best. Or write your own. Headlines and subheadings need not be complete sentences. They can be in the present tense.

Subheading	*Lane's ships return safely* *Savages destroy settlement* *Settlement plundered by natives*

Recount

No settlers came to meet our ships when we landed at Roanoke. The only prints in the sand were the bare footprints of the natives.

Picture

Caption

_____

The Beatles

 ## Literacy objectives

+ To make notes for a purpose. (Y5, T1: T27)
+ To construct sentences in different ways while retaining meaning. (Y5, T2: S8)
+ To develop skills of biographical writing. (Y6, T1: T14)
+ To proofread and edit own writing for clarity. (Y5, T1: S3)

 ## History objectives

(Unit 20)

+ To carry out personal research.
+ To extract information from reference material, including the Internet and CD-Roms.
+ To identify characteristic ideas in consumer marketing from the 1960s.

 ## Resources

+ Pictures of the Beatles from 1960 to 1970 and the individual members of the band to the present day (from a range of sources, including the Internet).
+ Video clips or sound recordings of the Beatles performing in the 1960s and present-day popular bands (for example, from the television programme 'Top of the Pops').
+ Records of the Beatles' songs from the 1960s.
+ A biographical dictionary.

 ## Starting point: Whole class

+ Show the children a video clip of the Beatles performing in the early 1960s or 70s. Discuss their performance. What do the children think about the band's image? Tell them about 'Beatlemania' – the almost hysterical reactions of teenagers to the Beatles.
+ Show the class a video clip of a performance by a present-day pop group. Ask the children what differences they notice between the Beatles and this modern band. Write their responses on the board or on a large sheet of paper under headings such as 'fashion' (clothes/ hairstyles/make-up), 'dancing', 'response to the performance', 'type of music', 'type of lyrics' and 'settings' (in which they performed).
+ Play records by other pop groups from the 1960s. Discuss the similarities and differences between past and present-day pop music recordings. Explain the terms '45', 'EP' and 'LP' and compare these vinyl records to the modern formats of cassettes and CDs.

 ## Using the photocopiable text

+ Enlarge the text on page 54 or make copies for each child. Explain that this is an extract from a biographical dictionary. It is about John Lennon, a member of the Beatles group. Show the children the biographical dictionary and explain that it contains entries for many different people. The one that contains the entry for John Lennon would also have entries for the other members of the group, their manager, Brian Epstein, as well as other pop groups. Discuss the term 'biographical' and what it means, compared with 'autobiographical'.
+ Share the text with the children. What does it tell us about John Lennon? Explain that many people use biographical dictionaries to find basic information about a person. They usually make notes as they are reading to help them to remember things about that person. Discuss why people may want to make notes from a biographical dictionary; for writing a magazine article, for instance. Discuss the process and format of note-making – do we use full sentences and punctuation? When might we need to make notes at school? Tell them that together they are going to make some notes about John Lennon.
+ Reread the first paragraph of the text together. Agree the main ideas and underline the key words, such as 'born', 'Liverpool', '9 October 1940', 'Quarry Bank High School', 'Liverpool College of Art' and 'Quarrymen'. Explain that these words would be useful for their notes. Point out that it is common, when writing notes, to use abbreviations for words, such as 'b' for 'born' and 'm' for 'married'. It is also acceptable to shorten words, such as Liverpool to L'pool. Show the children how the underlined words could be written as notes, for example:

      John Lennon b. L'pool, 9 Oct 1940
      Quarry Bank High, L'pool Coll. Art
      Band – Quarrymen

+ Continue in the same way for the next few (or all) of the paragraphs.
+ Now write on the board some notes, such as those about Brian Epstein on Activity sheet 1. Together, work to turn these notes into a biographical text with sentences.
+ Tell the children they are now going to work on an activity sheet and use a biographical extract to make notes and vice versa. Tell them they need to be careful with what they write and that they need to edit and proofread their work carefully.

The Beatles

 ## Group activities

Activity sheet 1: This is for children who can take a brief list of notes and rewrite them in biographical form. They have the advantage of having already done this exercise in the whole-class activity so should feel confident with the work. They then have to read a text and find the notes that can be made from it. Point out that it may help to delete conjunctions, such as 'but' and articles such as 'the' before they try to write the notes.

Activity sheet 2: This is for children who are beginning to use and make notes for a purpose. They should edit their writing to produce a polished final version. They can link sentences with simple connectives and use relative clauses beginning with 'that', 'which', 'who', 'whom', 'whose', 'when' or 'where'. They can recognise the distinctive features of brief biographical writing.

Activity sheet 3: This is for children who are competent in reading notes and using them to write sentences in a biographical style. They are given the additional challenge of using other sources to scan information for the most useful data, making notes for a purpose and filling out notes from more than one source into connected prose. They can link sentences with simple connectives and use relative clauses beginning with 'that', 'which', 'who', 'whom', 'whose', 'when' or 'where'. They can recognise the distinctive features of brief biographical writing and use them in their own writing. They can discuss their writing confidently with others and edit it to produce a polished final version of a given length.

 ## Plenary session

+ Invite the children to read out their notes and biographical details.
+ As a class, choose another person about whom to make biographical notes. This might be someone from the class, a teacher or adult helper or a famous person. Choose a scribe to ask for information about the person from the class and make notes about him or her on the board. Then, as a class, rewrite these notes in biographical style.

 ### Follow-up ideas for literacy

+ Encourage the children to talk to older members of their families and to read teenage literature from the 1960s to collect examples of old-fashioned words and phrases. Ask them to list expressions they use today which would not be understood by someone living in the 1960s.
+ Ask the children to research one of the band members from the Beatles. They should then complete a chart using the headings 'What do I know?', 'What do I think I know?' and 'What do I want to find out?' Help them to complete a fourth section entitled 'Where can I find out about it?'

+ Tell the children to use their notes from the completed chart to write a biography of one of the Beatles. Point out that the biography should be planned in chapters, for example, 'Childhood', 'Interest in music', 'Marriage and family', 'Meeting the other Beatles', 'First recordings', 'Fame', and 'The break-up of the Beatles and solo career'. Ask the children to record quotations to incorporate into the text and help them to develop skills in integrating speech with narrative.

 ### Follow-up ideas for history

+ The children could bring in memorabilia of the Beatles, such as records, posters, photographs, books and publicity material for a class display. Discuss what they have found out from the artefacts. Discuss any misconceptions, for example that mechanical gramophones were still in use and that Teddy boys were still in vogue.
+ Help the children to plan interviews with adults who lived throughout the 1960s and remember the Beatles. They could investigate the 'teen culture' which grew during that time.
+ Ask the class to produce a timeline about the Beatles with each child contributing different aspects of information about the members. They could add information about any significant events or news that they come across.

Lennon, John Winston, 1940 – 1980

English songwriter, singer and rhythm guitarist

Born in Liverpool on 9 October 1940, John Lennon was educated at Quarry Bank High School and Liverpool College of Art, where he formed a band, the Quarrymen.

In 1957 they performed at a church fête, where band-member Ivan Vaughan introduced his friend Paul McCartney to Lennon. McCartney joined the band, which changed its name to the Silver Beetles (later the Beatles).

George Harrison joined the Beatles for their 1960–61 tour of beat clubs in Hamburg, Germany. On their return to Liverpool Ringo Starr became their drummer.

They wrote their own songs, with John Lennon and Paul McCartney as the main songwriters, and performed regularly at the Cavern club in Liverpool. Their first Number One hit was 'Please Please Me' (1963).

In 1970 the Beatles split up. John Lennon had many solo hits, including 'Imagine' (1971).

He married Cynthia Powell, a fellow art student, in 1962 and they had a son, Julian (1963). They divorced. He married Yoko Ono, an artist, in 1969. Their son Sean was born in 1975.

John Lennon was shot dead outside his home in New York on 8 December 1980.

✦ Biographical dictionary ✦

✦ Read the notes below about Brian Epstein. Rewrite the notes in the style of a biographical dictionary.

- Brian Epstein had music store in Liverpool.
- Name of store was NEMS (North End Music Stores).
- NEMS had many requests for record called 'My Bonnie' by the Silver Beetles.
- Silver Beetles performed at Cavern Club.
- Brian Epstein went to club to listen to them.
- Became manager of band.

Use connectives, such as 'and' and words such as 'where', 'who' and 'which'.

_____

_____

_____

_____

_____

✦ Read the sentences below. They are written in the form of a biographical dictionary. Use the information to make a list of notes.

Born in Liverpool on 7 July 1940, Ringo Starr's real name was Richard Starkey. Because he always wore rings he was given the nickname Ringo. In 1957 he started a band, the Eddie Clayton Skiffle Group, with Eddie Miles, and was its drummer. Later in 1957 he joined the Raving Texans whose singer was Rory Storm. They became Rory Storm and the Hurricanes and in 1960 played in beat clubs in Hamburg, where Ringo met the Beatles.

_____

_____

_____

_____

_____

◆ Biographical dictionary ◆

◆ Read the notes below about Brian Epstein. Rewrite the
notes in the style of a biographical dictionary.

- Brian Epstein had music store in Liverpool.
- Name of store was NEMS.
- NEMS had many requests for record called 'My Bonnie'
  by the Silver Beetles.
- Silver Beetles performed at Cavern Club.
- Brian Epstein went to club to listen to them.
- Became manager of band.

_____

_____

_____

_____

_____

◆ Use the biographical dictionary entry for Paul McCartney to make notes.

Born in Liverpool on 18 June 1942, Sir Paul James McCartney was educated at the
Liverpool Institute High School. He learned to play the piano as a child, and then
began to learn the guitar at 14. He formed the band Wings in 1971 and produced the
UK's best-selling-ever single 'Mull of Kintyre' in 1977. In 1981 Wings were disbanded.
Paul founded the Liverpool Institute of Performing Arts in 1990, which was housed in
his old school, but now closed. He got a knighthood in 1997. Paul was married to
photographer Linda Eastman in 1969 (she died in 1998). They had two daughters,
Mary and Stella, and one son, James. Linda had her own daughter, Heather.

_____

_____

_____

_____

_____

_____

_____

Biographical dictionary

✦ Read the notes below about Paul McCartney. Rewrite the notes
in the style of a biographical dictionary.

Born Liverpool 18 June 1942. Name Sir Paul James McCartney. Educ: L'pool Institute
High Sch. Father in band (part-time) – Jim Mac's Jazz Band. Learned to play piano
as child. Began to learn guitar at 14. Formed band Wings '71. Made UK's best-
selling-ever single 'Mull of Kintyre' '77. Wings disbanded '81. Many solo hits inc
'Wonderful Christmastime' ('79). Founded ('90) Liverpool Inst of Performing Arts
(housed in his old sch, closed). Knighthood '97. m photographer Linda Eastman
1969 (d 1998) who had daughter, Heather. 2 daughters Mary & Stella, 1 son James.

_____

_____

_____

_____

_____

_____

_____

✦ Use information books and websites to find out about the life of George Harrison. Make
notes about his date and place of birth, education, significant hit records, other important
achievements, marriage and children. Write your notes here.

✦ Use your notes to write an entry about George Harrison for a biographical dictionary on the
back of this sheet. Edit your work to produce a final version.

The Indus Valley

 ## Literacy objectives

+ To revise language conventions and grammatical features of non-chronological reports. (Y6, T3: S1)
+ To write non-chronological reports linked to other subjects. (Y6, T1: T17)

 ## History objectives

(Unit 16)

+ To learn about the location of the Indus Valley civilisation.
+ To learn what was discovered in the Indus Valley.
+ To learn about the types of questions that can be answered from archaeological discoveries.

 ## Resources

+ Maps of the world and of India and Pakistan (showing the Indus Valley).
+ A timeline on which other periods (about which the children have learned) are indicated.
+ Pictures of the Indus Valley and surrounding plains.

 ## Starting point: Whole class

+ Help the class to find India and Pakistan on a map of the world. Ask the children if any of them have been to these countries. If so, what did they notice about the climate and the physical environment? Talk about the physical features that can be seen on the map, such as oceans, seas, mountains, valleys and rivers.
+ Look closely at a map of India and show the children the location of the Indus Valley. Show the class pictures of the Indus Valley area and talk about the climate there. Ask them why people might have chosen the Indus Valley and the plains around it for their settlements.
+ Point out the dates when people built cities in the Indus Valley area. Encourage the children to place these dates on the timeline. They could work out approximately how many years earlier it was than other periods they have studied.
+ Talk about the periods on the timeline about which we know the most, and where the gaps are. Show them BC and AD on the timeline and explain that, although they are terms related to Christianity, historians recognise them as standard terms for dates.

 ## Using the photocopiable text

+ Make a copy of the class text (page 60) for each child. Read the passage with the children and discuss the way in which it is structured. They could summarise what each paragraph is about and its purpose. For example, paragraph 1 introduces the topic and informs the reader of time and place; paragraph 2 describes the main features of the archaeological site and gives the archaeologists' interpretations of them; paragraphs 3 and 4 describe smaller features and some of the observations made; and paragraph 5 gives a summary of what happened to the city.
+ Discuss the type of language used in the text. It has an impersonal style and is a non-chronological report (it does not contain connectives that indicate the passage of time, such as 'then', 'next' or 'after that'). Ask the children to identify verbs in the past tense and present tense and to explain why each tense is used. For example, the present tense is used to describe the things that have been found and still exist in the Indus Valley. The past is used to describe the things that archaeologists have found in the recent past.
+ Tell the children that they are going to write reports about the city of Lothal. Those doing Activity sheets 1 and 2 will be asked to identify facts that are relevant to the report and rewrite the report using them. Those doing Activity sheet 3 will be writing a report based on the whole-class text.

 ## Group activities

Activity sheet 1: This is for children who are beginning to recognise the style of the language of non-chronological reports. By providing a text which has parts which 'do not fit', the activity sheet helps them to focus on the differences between appropriate and inappropriate styles. They are beginning to recognise inconsistent use of tenses.

Activity sheet 2: This is similar to Activity sheet 1 but contains more text to work with, therefore requiring a longer report to be written.

Activity sheet 3: This is for children who understand the features of non-chronological reports and are beginning to use them in their own writing. They are developing their skills in using tenses consistently.

The Indus Valley

 Plenary session

✦ Invite the children who completed Activity sheet 1 to point out the parts that they think do not belong to the report, and to explain why they do not belong. The others could add any they miss. Did they spot any incorrect tenses? Ask them if the report needs to have the same tense throughout, when the tense can change and why. If they had difficulty with this, invite the others to help them.

Select some of the children who completed Activity sheet 2 to read out their reports, while the others listen for correct and incorrect use of tenses. Did they organise their report in a logical way? Make an enlarged copy (or overhead transparency) of Activity sheet 3 and invite the children who completed the sheet to read out their responses. Write the most appropriate responses on the copy.

 Follow-up ideas for literacy

✦ The children could find out how beads were made at Lothal (this is known, because beads are still made using the same ancient methods). Revise the features of instructional texts and ask the children to use a flow chart to plan a set of instructions for making the beads, and then to write the instructions in the imperative form, using diagrams where necessary. Help them to edit their work. How well did they help the reader to follow the instructions? Did they give the text a heading and show a picture of the finished product? Did they include a list of equipment and materials at the beginning of the text? Were the instructions sequenced correctly, step-by-step?

✦ Ask the children to consider the purpose of the water tank at Lothal, the reason the buildings were on earthen platforms or the purpose of the wall around the city. They could collect more information about Lothal and use it to form an argument about the different explanations. They could write an argument between two archaeologists with different views – this could be presented as a conversation; or they could write an argument which presents different views and summarise it to express their own view.

 Follow-up ideas for history

✦ Help the children to find out about the different archaeologists who have studied the Indus Valley at different times and how opinions changed as discoveries were made. They could brainstorm the kinds of things archaeologists can and cannot find out from excavations.

✦ Explain that an important aspect of archaeological work is the discussion and research which goes on before and after the excavation, to link what is discovered to existing knowledge and to use the technology available to learn as much as possible about the finds.

✦ Provide pictures or colour slides of artefacts found in Lothal and other areas of the Indus Valley and ask the children what they can learn from the artefacts. For example, inscriptions have been found on pottery and seals from the Indus Valley and, although these cannot be understood, what can the children learn about the people who lived in the Indian sub-continent more than 4,000 years ago (when people in Europe were living in caves and had no cities or written language and only primitive tools)?

◆ Lothal ◆

Archaeologists who excavated the Indus Valley and its surrounding plains in Pakistan and India in the twentieth century discovered the remains of several ancient cities. One of these was Lothal, which is thought to have been built in about 2400BC. It was on an area of high ground on the banks of the river Sabarmati, which empties into the Gulf of Khambhat. The river has since changed its course.

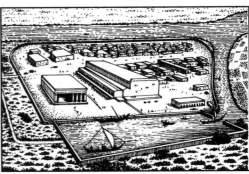

Around the city was a 13-metre-thick wall and just outside the eastern wall was a huge water tank (1), dating from about 2350BC and measuring about 37 metres from east to west, nearly 220 metres from north to south and more than 4 metres deep. It extended from the river and along the whole length of the town. Leading off the river into the tank was an inlet channel 1.7 metres above the bottom of the tank. Some archaeologists think that this tank was a dock, since much evidence was found that Lothal was a centre of manufacture and trade. Others think it was a reservoir.

Within the walls was a large citadel or acropolis (2) built on an earthen platform just under 130 metres long and just over 60 metres wide. It had a row of twelve baths on the southern side, with outlet channels which joined the main drain (3) leading into the tank. Within the citadel were rows of houses. To the south of the citadel are the remains of a warehouse (4). The buildings were constructed from skillfully-made kiln-fired bricks of regular sizes, and the bricks from which the baths were made had polished surfaces and fitted together tightly; no water could seep through them.

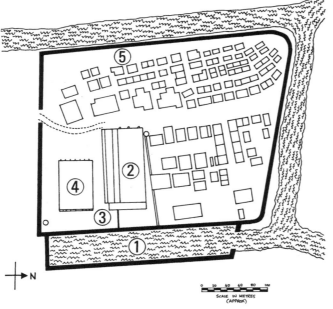

In the lower town, with its streets running from east to west, the remains were found of rows of houses, all with drains, built on earthen platforms. In the remains of some houses were a well and a kitchen. Also in the lower town, separate from the residential area, was a commercial area in which the remains of a coppersmith's workshop and pot furnaces were found. On the edge of the commercial area archaeologists found a workshop area so large that it was more like a factory (5); it had eleven rooms (surrounding a courtyard) which included workers' quarters, a warehouse and guardrooms, and a kiln with twisted chambers made from mud-plastered bricks. This was the main bead factory. Examples of beautiful tiny beads had already been found in different parts of the Indus Valley.

The city of Lothal was flooded in about 1900BC and was abandoned.

✦ Writing a report ✦

- ✦ The purpose of the report below is to describe some of the artefacts found by archaeologists at Lothal.
- ✦ Underline the parts that do not belong in the report and circle any tenses that are wrong.

> When archaeologists excavated Lothal on the plains around the Indus Valley, they found a complete set of games pieces. The pieces look as if they are for playing a game like chess. We saw a television programme about Lothal at school yesterday. The games pieces reminded the archaeologists of others found in a tomb in Egypt. We saw a programme about Egypt, too. Some of the pieces are shaped like animals, some like castles and some like pyramids with an ivory handle.
>
> At Lothal and other sites stones were found which archaeologists think were used like marbles. We play marbles in the playground.
>
> This evidence tells us that the people of Lothal have leisure time. They do not just work, eat and sleep.

- ✦ Rewrite the report as it should be written. Continue on the other side if you need to.

_____

_____

_____

_____

_____

_____

_____

◆ Writing a report ◆

✦ The purpose of the report below is to describe some of the artefacts found by archaeologists at Lothal.

✦ Underline the parts that do not belong in the report and circle any tenses that are wrong.

When archaeologists excavated Lothal on the plains around the Indus Valley, they found a complete set of games pieces. The pieces look as if they are for playing a game like chess. We saw a television programme about Lothal at school yesterday. The games pieces reminded the archaeologists of others found in a tomb in Egypt. We saw a programme about Egypt, too. Some of the pieces are shaped like animals, some like castles and some like pyramids with an ivory handle.

The archaeologists found other games pieces, including some dice. They have markings on them which are different from modern dice but similar to others found in the Indus Valley. We are going to see a programme about the other sites next week. I am looking forward to it.

At Lothal and other sites stones were found which archaeologists think were used like marbles. We play marbles in the playground.

This evidence tells us that the people of Lothal have leisure time. They do not just work, eat and sleep.

✦ Rewrite the report as it should be written. Continue on the other side if you need to.

_____

_____

_____

_____

_____

_____

_____

◆ Writing a report ◆

◆ Use the text about Lothal in the Indus Valley to help you write a report. Fill in all the gaps below with relevant information. Use the correct tense for your verbs.

Archaeologists who excavated _____ in _____

in the _____ century discovered the remains of _____

_____

The site dates from _____

On the site the archaeologists also found _____

_____

_____

> Begin by describing the large features and then the smaller ones.

From this they can tell that _____

_____

_____

> Write about what archaeologists think about the remains.

There were also remains of _____

_____

_____

_____

> Describe what can be seen there. Give some measurements.

The site is important because _____

_____

_____

It_____

_____

_____

> Say when the site stopped being used or how it changed.

Chapter 1

The Victorian web www.telematics.ex.ac.uk/virvic/
Her Benny by Silas Hocking, Memories Paperbacks, 1994 (first published 1880)
London Labour and the London Poor, Volume II, Henry Mayhew, Dover, 1986 (first published 1861)
Language Glossaries (a series of mini-books on dialects: for example, *Lancashire English* and *Rhyming Cockney Slang*), Abson Books, London

Chapter 2

Sources of paintings
'Children at Play' (John Dawson Watson), Private Collection (in *Victorian Painters,* by Jeremy Maas, Barrie & Jenkins, 1969
'Bubbles' (Sir John Everett Millais), owned by Lever Brothers, on permanent loan to the Royal Academy, London
'Her Idol' (W Q Orchardson), Manchester City Art Galleries
'The Lowther Arcade' (H C Bryant), Coutts & Co
'The Garden Seat' (Kate Greenaway), Royal Albert Memorial Museum, Exeter

Museums
National Museum of Childhood, Bethnal Green (London) www.vam.ac.uk/vastatic/nmc/index.html
National Museum of Childhood, Beaumaris, Anglesey www.nwi.co.uk/museumofchildhood/index.htm

Chapter 3

Darlington Railway Centre and Museum, North Road Station, Darlington, DL3 6ST, 01325 460532

Chapter 5

BBC History www.bbc.co.uk/history/
'The Origins of Everyday Things', Reader's Digest, 1998
The Daily Mail Centenary CD-Rom (Educational Edition), Daily Mail, 1996

Chapter 6

The Oxford Concise Dictionary of English Etymology, 1986
The Shorter Oxford Dictionary
Dictionary of Word Origins, Linda & Rogers Flavell, Kyle Cathie, 1996

Chapter 7

The British Museum www.thebritishmuseum.ac.uk/
Useful reference for teachers, for Greek words and characters: *Learn Ancient Greek,* Peter Jones, Duckworth, 1998. You can find all the Greek characters on the symbol menu in Microsoft Word. Peter Jones's book tells you which is which.
Encyclopaedia Britannica www.Britannica.com

Chapter 8

National Park Service of the USA at Fort Raleigh historical centre on Roanoke http://www.nps.gov/fora/
The American Colonists' Library http://www.nationalcenter.org/ColonyofRoanoke.html
Principal Navigations, Voyages of the English Nation III, (Richard Hakluyt, 1600), Penguin, 1972

Chapter 9

For information and brief biographies of pop singers: www.rollingstone.com/artists/
The Virgin Encyclopedia of Popular Music, Colin Larkin, Virgin Books, 1999

Chapter 10

A websites with information about the Indus Valley: www.harappa.com/lothal/index.html